POST COMMUNIST CAPITALISM and CAPITAL:

Foreign Investors in Transitional Economies

POST COMMUNIST CAPITALISM and CAPITAL:

Foreign Investors in Transitional Economies

Tauno Tiusanen

NOVA SCIENCE PUBLISHERS, INC.
Commack

Art Director: Maria Ester Hawrys
Assistant Director: Elenor Kallberg
Graphics: Denise Dieterich, Kerri Pfister,
Erika Cassatti and Barbara Minerd
Manuscript Coordinator: Sharyn Schweidel
Book Production: Tammy Sauter, Benjamin Fung
Circulation: Irene Kwartiroff and Annette Hellinger

Library of Congress Cataloging-in-Publication Data
available upon request

ISBN 1-56072-301-7

1996 Nova Science Publishers, Inc.
6080 Jericho Turnpike, Suite 207
Commack, New York 11725
Tele. 516-499-3103 Fax 516-499-3146
E Mail Novasci1@aol.com

Printed in the United States of America

CONTENTS

ACKNOWLEDGEMENT

I want to express my gratitude to my wife, Ritva, who has helped me with my archive and selected material for my rsearch. I also give my thanks to Mrs Kay McWalter who deciphered my hand-written manuscript. Mr Richard Berry, of the Institute of Russian and East European Studies at Glasgow University has commented on my text. Thanks to his effort and his knoweledge on the subject, the book has reached a readable form.

Tauno Tiusanen

26 November 1993

INTRODUCTION

In the early stage of Soviet power, economic discussion was focused on one particular question: how could the first socialist state accumulate the capital necessary for industrialization? Eventually it was decided that the capital needed for the systemic change - to turn a predominately agricultural society into an industrialized one - would have to come from internal sources through 'forced savings'. Extensive investment programmes were drawn up by the central planning office and the industrialization programme begun.

Ambitious investment programmes became an obsession in Soviet-type economies. The traditional ideology of socialism ridiculed the Western capitalist principle of spontaneity, in which economic growth relies on savings made by independent economic units and individuals who are free to make investment decisions. Socialist economists pointed out that savings and investment decisions must be concentrated in the hands of central bureaucrats, otherwise business cycles could never be avoided.

Communist rulers in all Soviet-type economies became obsessed with investment. They thought that increments in capital stock would ultimately produce a cornucopia, or lead to a heaven on earth. In order to achieve high figures of overall economic growth, they kept the share of GNP in investment at a constantly high level . At the same time, in this system of over-investment, efficiency criteria were extremely vague or non-existent. Maintenance of capital stock was neglected and quality considerations were of secondary importance only.

It is ironic that now, in the post-communist period, transitional economies (TEs) which have had very extensive investment programmes for about half a century (or in the Soviet case, even longer) need a long investment boom in order to transform their economies from the communist smoke stack era into post-industrial service economies. In the process many hopelessly outdated operations must simply be abandoned.

A 'shock therapy', similar to that employed in the communist industrialization drive, is required. A wave of investments must occur before overall living standards can improve. Once more the question must be asked: Where is the money needed for investments supposed to come from? Again, the populace is asked to make sacrifices in the area of consumption in order to create a bright future.

The immediate post-communist shock has brought about a severe slump in economic activity. This is only natural given the communist legacy; many former operations are not worth transforming. Also, with overall living standards deteriorating in quantitative terms (availability and quality of goods have shown an improvement), it can be assumed that TEs have a low propensity to save and, thus, the ability to accumulate capital. In order to modernise, therefore, it is of utmost importance for TEs to have access to outside sources of finance, during the early phases of transition. External sources of money can theoretically be tapped in three different ways.

First, there is the option given to TEs to take large-scale loans from international financial markets. Unfortunately, many TEs inherited a heavy debt burden from the communist period. Therefore, TEs have only limited creditworthiness (with very clear differences between each country). Some international organizations like the IMF and the World Bank offer special credit allocations, but these are always rigidly conditional. No great aid package along the lines of the Marshall Plan - which helped post-war Western Europe - is in the pipe-line.

Secondly, TEs can try to attract portfolio-investments from outside. With the privatization of post-communist assets, secondary markets in securities have come into being. Shares in these 'newly emerging post-communist markets' tend to be very inexpensive for foreign investors. The relative 'undervaluation' of TE currencies is one factor behind this phenomenon. In autumn 1994 it was widely stated that shares in Russia were available for just one per cent of their 'real value'. At the same time, it is difficult to establish what is the 'real value' of TE shares. International investors certainly know that newly established stock exchanges in TEs are extremely volatile. Therefore, high risks, but at the same time, huge potential gains are available for portfolio investors in TEs.

The third possibility is that of obtaining foreign direct investments (FDIs) to help modernize TE economies. In this book FDIs are defined as strategic investments by foreign economic agents who enter the TE market by acquiring (partially or wholly) local enterprises. There is also the possibility of making a 'greenfield investment' in the host country.

FDIs have had an interesting but not yet substantial impact in the economic development of TEs. One of the reasons for this is the fact that TEs have experienced a severe slump during the first post-communist years. Obviously, political and economic stability has not been properly established in the TE region as a whole. At the same time, TEs offer an historic opportunity for multinational companies which were reluctant to invest directly in the East during the communist era.

It can be assumed that FDIs in TEs will increase considerably during the second half of the 1990s when growth prospects in TEs are expected to improve. At the same time, TEs are obviously competing with each other to receive FDIs. In this competition, there will be losers and winners: FDIs will concentrate on those TEs with a favourable 'investment climate' comprised of political and economic stability and reasonable growth prospects. FDIs in TEs show an uneven distribution which is likely to continue: those TEs with a clear commitment to economic transition will be favoured by foreign investors; TEs which hesitate to reform and revitalise their economies will have difficulties attracting foreign companies.

FDIs also have significant indirect effects on the changing economies in TEs. Western companies that establish operations in a post-centralized, monopolistic TE, contribute to the emergence of competition, and the dynamism thus created facilitates the ending of the inertia inherent in Soviet-type economies.

However, there is also a risk that state-owned monopolies will be replaced by private ones, some of which will be in foreign control. There are already complaints in TEs which accuse foreign companies of cherry-picking; by acquiring the best TE assets cheaply and then attracting the best of the local labour, leaving local companies in disadvantageous positions with regard to competition. The sale of the local 'family silver' to foreigners is often said to have features of neocolonialism.

It is not possible here to analyse the validity of this argument with regard to the various TEs. However, the striking success by ex-communist political parties, in the elections in various TEs, highlight the fact that 'shock therapy' tactics for economic transition are not wholly appreciated by the local electorate. One clear aspect of discontent is the growing influence of Western companies which necessarily cause a cultural shock for locals.

This short book on FDIs in TEs does not try to give a comprehensive picture of all aspects of the 'invasion' of foreign companies in post-communist countries. Continued research will be required before we can fully understand the impact of the new phenomenon of FDIs in TEs and the possibilities engendered by the emerging business cultures.

Chapter One

1. The Legacy of Communism

> People show particular interest in the socio-economic and political system of existing socialism, which has become established in a large group of countries occupying over a quarter of the globe. Almost one-third of the earth's population live in socialist countries, which produce over 40 per cent of the world's industrial output, 57 per cent of the coal, 35 per cent of the steel, 45 per cent of cotton fabrics and 44 per cent of woollen cloths, harvest 39 per cent of the world's grain, 67 per cent of potato and 41 per cent of cotton crops... The USSR attained a leading place in social economic scientific and technological progress; it has also liquidated crises and unemployment and gained unquestionable supremacy in economic growth rates; all these factors attest to the advantages of the Soviet economic system and its managerial methods.

These lines were written by Leonid Abalkin[1] at the turn of the 1970s and 1980s. In the late 1980s, this well-known economist became Minister of Economics in the Soviet government. At that time a group of eminent economists

[1]Leonid Abalkin, *The Economic System of Socialism*, Moscow, 1980, p.7.

started working on a new economic scheme, which was published in 1990 and came to be known as 'the 500-days programme' or 'the Shatalin plan' (termed in Russia: *Perekhod k rynku*). This important report on the Soviet economy was never accepted as a guideline for economic policy, but it listed the most important flaws of the economic system:

> The economic and political instability that the country (Soviet Union) is undergoing should not be viewed as an ordinary crisis which may be surmounted by using the internal reserves of the system... The lack of vitality has been masked up to the present by the extensive use of human and natural resources, but this type of economic development exhausted itself back in the 1960s... The country's economy has found itself deprived of mechanisms for revitalisation. The gap in the level of technology, quality of goods and living standards (by a factor of 3-5) with OECD countries has reached critical proportions... Since the mid-1970s, the national economy has functioned for the most part by using the income from exports of raw materials and energy, limitation of consumption, and isolation from the world market. In the 1980s, practically no economic growth was observed and squandering of the national wealth occurred. The production apparatus has not renewed itself in most sectors for 15-25 years, soil fertility in a number of regions has decreased by a factor of 2-3, natural resources have been used in a predatory manner, and the burden on the environment in a number of regions has exceeded all acceptable limits. A beggarly standard of living for tens of millions of people, the impossibility of satisfying critical needs, and the absence of incentives to work have given rise to a process of physical and social degradation.

There is a striking difference between these two citations. What had happened during the 1980s in the 'socialist camp' to take it from the apparently fully confident time of the early 1980s? In the middle of the 1980s the oil price suddenly collapsed. Although this did have a negative affect the balance of trade of the Soviet Union, for such an economy, with its high degree of autarchy, this was not a decisive blow. In fact, centrally planned economies withered away because of their own internal weaknesses. The most severe of these was the inability to minimize costs and maximize efficiency.

The traditional, centrally planned system divided the economy into bureaucratic units called industrial ministries; a model adopted throughout the CMEA[2] area. In this system each of these bureaucratic units defended its own territory and emphasised its own importance. This was of great significance to economic development in a situation where budgetary limits were loosely defined. Also, it was the characteristic of this system to over-invest; with extremely vague or non-existent criteria of efficiency. In such economies there were numerous investment projects where work was started, but never finished.

The selfish principle of looking after your own patch prohibited a logical allocation of work between a ministry and the organizations working under its rule. Autarchy had taken over. For example, plastic and metal needs were manufactured in the production plants of each region, because the units specializing in these particular materials under another ministry did not deliver to their neighbours.

---

[2]CMEA = Council of Mutual Economic Assistance: the trading bloc of communist countries better known as Comecon in the West.

In addition to investment failures, a long chain of overlapping investments coud be observed.

The well-known Russian writer, Sergei Salygin, gives us an interesting example of what happens when people are preoccupied with their own economic area. For years, the water ministry studied the possibility of making the Siberian rivers flow in the direction of the southern farmlands. People from 185 organizations were involved in the planning stage of this massive project, and the total number involved under the Ministry's directions rose at one point to 68,000. There was great reluctance to reveal the costs incurred in the planning process, but Salygin gives an estimate of approximately one billion rubles.[3]

The project, which would have changed the climatic conditions of the globe if carried into effect, was eventually dropped. Naturally, the Ministry was unwilling to admit its failure. Salygin wonders why a project which could not have been implemented for less than 100 billion rubles had captivated the Ministry so much in the first place. It would hardly have had any significance for the foodstuffs industry; better results at significantly lower cost could have been achieved by improving methods of transportation, packaging and storage. However, the idea of financial accountability is alien to the bureaucratic workings of these ministries.

In the bureaucratic command economy, the idea of using profit in the marketplace as an indicator of corporate success was dismissed for ideological reasons. However, entrepreneurship as such could not be discarded completely. It was necessary to concoct new yardsticks to

---

[3]*Novy mir*, No.1/87.

measure the success of business organizations which were bound to the economic will of the central government.

These yardsticks were geared to measuring, in a reasonably simple manner, how well the organizations had met the quotas set for them by centrally made plans which determined material input and output. The economic planners had to know what resources were going into an organization and what products were coming out in return.

In a traditional planned economy, an economic indicator called gross production was used for measuring the success of an organization. This shows output, not only by unit, by ton or by metre but also in terms of monetary value. At various time, different socialist countries have tried out numerous other indicators, but the belief in gross production has maintained its dominant position with astonishing resilience.

Economists in both the East and the West agree unanimously that using the gross production indicator has been injurious to the economic development of the centrally planned societies. Nevertheless, no other solution was found for this problem in the Soviet era.

Several problems arise when gross production is used as an indicator:

- Cost awareness becomes obscured in organizations. When the price of factors of production such as energy are kept artificially low, production costs are not taken into consideration in the struggle to meet production quotas. There is no competition to exert pressures on cost.
- It is the primary concern of both the organization and the industrial ministry to find enough resources to meet

the quotas. As a result, there is constant excess demand for raw materials, semi-finished products, machinery and labour. Organizations as well as ministries over-estimate their needs and thus hoard what they need for production. This transmits an indirect signal of a need for further investment in the production of raw materials, semi-finished goods and machinery.

- Success measured by gross production induces the manufacture of goods which are not in demand. It is typical of a planned system to think that once a good has been manufactured it can also be charged regardless of its usefulness. Manufacturing in excess of demand is an integral part of production based on set quotas, and has caused immeasurable welfare losses.
- The system of gross production indicators has a very poor application to other industries except basic manufacturing. The application of the model to the construction industry results in no one being interested in final outcomes. According to Shmelev[4], the implementation of construction projects takes on average over ten years in the Soviet Union, ten times longer than in the West. As to the service industries, this kind of mentality leads to complete illogicality. For example, when mileage driven is taken as a basis for assessing the transportation industry, it makes it less attractive to carry an actual load on the return journey. Restaurants can make the food inedible if the company pigsty can be sustained on leftovers. Quotas are a serious impediment to the conversion from an industrial economy to

---

[4]*Novy mir*, No.6/1987

a post-industrial service society. The planning of services is difficult, as is its control.

- Traditional gross production philosophy has an inbuilt propensity to cause consummate environmental disaster. Plant managers whose hands are tied by production quotas are not at all interested in any kind of toxic emissions reduction as long as they are having to meet strict quantitative output requirements. Moreover, the system creates constant excess demand for intermediate goods such as chemicals and metals whose production is particularly pollutive.
- The maintenance of national industrial resources and infrastructure are of secondary importance in a system relying on gross production. It is difficult to estimate the astronomical extra cost caused to the economy by such attitudes. In the winter of 1990, *Izvestia* published an article predicting a chain of disasters caused by the extensive decay of buildings. The article had been motivated by the explosion of a gas pipe which had caused great damage.
- When quantity is the key indicator of efficiency, the quality of goods is seen as immaterial. Plant managers see innovation and product development as a burden, hampering their efforts to meet the quotas. This results in poor commercial exploitation of inventions. The one exception is the military establishment which has traditionally functioned as a privileged sector, though it has been kept in isolation from the rest of the economy.

During the Soviet Communist Party conference in the summer of 1988, Gorbachev vented his anger upon those opposing *perestroika*:

> The use of output quotas has been able to continue solely thanks to ministries and planners opposing reform. It is totally irresponsible to force organizations to produce goods to meet not demand but impressive quota figures. How does it pay us to increase the production of raw materials and fuels if they are swallowed up by an irrational and wasteful use of resources? Who is to benefit from the increased supply of farm machinery if no one wants these machines because of their poor performance? Light industry should not be concerned with production quotas, but with producing goods which satisfy the needs of consumers.[5]

Aleksandr Gelman, a novelist and dramatist, very aptly damned the gross production indicator when he wrote:

> 'The notorious antiparameter called gross production is suffocating our economy. It has deluded us all, dazzled us with its deceptively simple and clear-cut principles: the heaver, longer and dearer, the better. It has been nice and easy to manage by using production quotas. It has created a generation of plant managers who, by exaggerating the volumes of production, have legally exploited the system to improve their own career prospects... The day we rid ourselves for good of this production indicator mentality should be marked as a national day of liberation, and it should be celebrated annually as a warning to generations to come. And this is a serious proposal.'[6]

That Gorbachev took a stand over the continuing dominance of the production quotas at that point of time

---

[5] Offene Worte: Gorbatschow, Ligatschow, Jelzin und 4991 Delegierete diskutieren über den richtigen Weg, Sowjetunion, Sommer 1988, ECHO-Dokumentation, Augsburg, July 1988.

[6] *Literaturnaya gazeta*, September 10, 1986.

is interesting. Presumably, in the summer of 1988 he saw how the first three years of his reforms had come to nothing, so now he chose political advisers with distinctly more radical economic views. In the autumn of 1990, however, the Soviet Union still missed out on the change of radical reform; the small CMEA countries, meanwhile, had begun to tear down the basic structures of their centrally planned societies.

When we examine the period of transition in the centrally planned economies, we must keep in mind the different resources of those economies. The Soviet Union was able to hold on to its bureaucratic system based on production quotas because of the immense amount of raw materials it possessed. The lavish spending of economic resources connected with this system has not, however, been as easily justified in those countries which are not so rich in raw materials. The small CMEA countries reached a point where the idea of expansive, extravagant growth virtually met its absolute physical limit. The traditional centrally planned economy was driven to a complete dead end.

In the autumn of 1990, the Vienna Institute for Comparative Economic Studies estimated that energy equalling 600 million tons of oil was being wasted every year in the former CMEA area. This much energy could have been saved if the efficiency rate of energy consumption in Eastern Europe could have been raised to Western levels. The amount was roughly equal to the annual oil production of the Soviet Union.[7]

---

[7]T Balabanov and R Dietz: 'Eastern and East-West Energy Prospects' in P Havlik (ed): *Dismantling the Command Economy in Eastern Europe*. The Vienna Institute for Comparative Economic Studies, Yearbook III. Boulder-San Francisco-Oxford, 1991.

Per unit of GDP, the Soviet Union used 210 per cent more steel, 180 per cent more fertilizers, 200 per cent more cotton and 160 per cent more cement than the United States. Similar comparisons show that irrational use of primary products in centrally planned economies have been made quite frequently in recent years. Gorbachev's previously quoted remark, in which he questioned the sense of increasing the production of primary and intermediate products if the increase ends up being wasted, may well be justified.[8]

As to the problems of the construction industry in centrally planned economies, they have proved insuperable. Whilst the various industrial ministries hoarded investments in their own sectors, the construction industry was in a constant state of overheating. The average completion time for construction projects was more than ten years, and the fact that some projects were never completed reflects a particular failure of the investment policy.

It has been estimated that several billion rubles' worth of imported machinery was lying about unused in the Soviet Union. Because of the prevailing shortage of western currencies, the needs of the national economy are supposed to be vetted thoroughly before decisions on imports are taken; but serious mistakes are also made in this sector.

Agriculture and central planning have been extremely difficult to operate in concert. In the Soviet Union, agricultural investments have accounted for over one quarter (27-28 per cent) of the annual total investments of the national economy. The corresponding figure for the United States is 3-4 per cent. According to academician Vladimir

---

[8]*Sosialismin teoria*, No.43/1990.

Tikhonov, producing one ruble's worth of food today requires an investment of almost 5 rubles. Agriculture in the Soviet Union receives about five times more tractors and eleven times more combine harvesters than agriculture in the US, which produces about 50 per cent more grain than the Soviet Union. Only about one half of the record-breaking harvest of 1990 was usable, due to faulty harvesting, transport and storage systems.[9]

Foreign trade fits very poorly into the traditional model of a planned economy. Central planners first define the resources that the economy already has, then they decide what it is that can be done with these given resources. Prices are fixed in advance. With such a system, foreign trade is a risk factor the effects of which cannot be controlled by the planners in advance. Thus, it is understandable that efforts have been made to minimize the risks involved in foreign trade. Some literature on the subject has gone as far as proposing that foreign trade should be eliminated completely and that the economy should aim at complete self sufficiency. This would guarantee that cyclical changes in the world market would not disturb the work of the planners.

Naturally enough, in centrally planned economies foreign trade is strictly controlled by state monopolies. In the Soviet Union, this arrangement became established quite soon after the Revolution, in the spring of 1918. The idea of using state monopolies for foreign trade is based on the primacy of imports. When the Soviet Union became a sovereign state, the concentration of external means of payment into the government's hands was considered appropriate to enable the nation to use the money to buy the

---

[9] *Business in the USSR*. No.4/1990.

machinery essential for the country's industrial revolution. Nevertheless, exports were traditionally regarded an unfortunate necessity, an act of giving up important resources which would actually be needed in the home country.

From its very beginning, the state monopoly fulfilled the protectionist needs. According to Lenin, the tariffs generally used in foreign trade were not sufficient for protecting the new socialist industry from foreign competition. However, history has proved that the socialist system did not fail: protection was, indeed, very efficient.

In many respects, the state monopoly of foreign trade worked well in the Soviet Union. The 'negative' side of foreign trade - exports - was conducted, without any particular trouble, through the sale of raw materials. Some structural changes took place: for a time, considerable quanitities of foodstuffs were exported and when the surplus in this area had been depleted they were replaced by energy exports. Although such overseas marketing brought astronomical gains during the two energy crises, these benefits can only be considered windfall profits.

The situation in the small CMEA countries was not so favourable as that in the Soviet Union. Where there is a lack of raw materials in the domestic market, more products have to be imported and the chance to generate external means of payment is lost. In order to export, therefore, much attention has to be given to the competitiveness of final products. During the Soviet era trade with the Soviet Union guaranteed sufficient affordable imports and a market for exports.

Although the other CMEA countries differed considerably from the Soviet Union in size and resources, their economies were all forced into the same Stalinist mould after the Second World War. As in the Marxist growth model, heavy industry was to form the backbone of each of these socialist economies.

The Soviet Union was very close to complete self sufficiency before the Second World War. Great quantities of machinery and equipment had been imported as a first stage and then copied in the new Soviet manufacturing plants. After the war it was thought that the model of self sufficiency could be carried out at a regional level: the socialist economic space could become self sufficient, a bloc independent of the West.

A unique kind of 'dual protectionism' was established for the intersocialist division of labour. On the one hand, the state monopoly of each socialist country protected its own developing industries from external competition, but on the other hand, the small CMEA countries did not have to worry about the marketing of their new industrial goods because demand from the immense Soviet market was limitless. The Soviet Union paid for these goods with raw materials and energy, thus guaranteeing the supply of these products to the CMEA area.

The distinctive features of the system were bilateral trade and clearing accounts, the weaknesses of which started to emerge as early as the 1950s. With each country concentrating on heavy industry, overlapping structures soon resulted. Not enough attention was paid to the individual country's comparative advantages or the competitiveness of manufactured products. Consequently, there was already an over-supply of certain machinery in the 1960s, whilst at the same time it was becoming clear that there was a lack of primary products.

These problems were discussed seriously at the beginning of the 1960s. It was thought that, for ideological reasons, it was not possible to improve economic-socialist integration by means of free market methods. The possibility of supranational planning to enhance integration was eventually taken into consideration. Based on such possibilities, draft proposals were put forward to set up a division of labour which would be flexible enough to adapt to the natural potential of each member nation.

The less developed European CMEA countries, particularly Romania, disapproved strongly of these proposals. Romania believed that each socialist country should have its own national plan directing the country in accordance with Marxist growth models. Because no common socialist production assets existed, no supranational economic planning could take place either. Hence the idea was dropped, and the overlapping development of economic structures was continued.

To some extent an integration process among the CMEA countries was carried out independently of both theoretical models. This was based on neither the free market economy, nor on supra-national planning, but on mutual reliance which was sustained through bilateral trade agreements.

The weaknesses of the system became obvious in the 1970s when the dual protectionism within the CMEA area deprived these economies of the chance to keep up with the technological progress of the rest of the world. Hence it became clear that eventually the doors to foreign trade with the West had to be opened.

At that time in Eastern Europe, it was still generally thought that the competition between economic systems would end in the victory of socialism. Nevertheless, it was recognised that the prevailing system needed to be strengthened by a new element that had been lacking: Western technology. It was believed that this element could easily be fitted into the centrally planned economy.

The strategy had, in many respects, a good chance of survival. Post-war reconstruction in Western Europe was over and companies were looking for new markets. The first oil crisis led to a situation where new investment opportunities had to be found for petro-dollars.

In effect, trade between East and West boomed. There was demand for Western technology in the East, and purchases could be paid for through international funding. The rosy period ended, however, in the late 1970s. The lack of competitiveness of the CMEA countries could not be cured by purchases of technology, and the massive foreign lending had reached its limits. Added to this was the fact that the crisis in Afghanistan brought restrictions on technology transfer for political reasons.

It has often been claimed in retrospect that it was specifically the problems with foreign trade which held back modern and rational development in Eastern Europe. The purchases of Western technology in the 1970s had brought about the illusion that modernization of planned economies could take place without changing the system. In reality, for the most part, the benefits of Western machinery had failed to materialize within the socialist managerial environment.

Nevertheless, the economies were still thriving because rising energy prices resulted in an increased demand for the products of these countries from the Soviet Union. However, the small CMEA countries hardly had a chance to enjoy the benefits of their burgeoning economies. It was not long before higher prices of energy, together with the cost of servicing the debt incurred with the West, was limiting the possibilities of improving the standard of living. The gap between the living standards of the East and the West became even wider in the late 1980s.

The one party system had earlier been justified by the claim that the communist party could guarantee the best possible standard of living for everyone. However, as the standard of living slumped in the 1980s, such a claim became absurd. The changing situation in the Soviet Union in the post-Brezhnevian period became an important factor in subverting the one party regime in 1989. The opposers of reform could no longer count on the support of the Soviet Union as they had during the Prague Spring of 1968.

In the West, it is often claimed that the Soviet Union exploited the East European countries economically, and that this triggered the 'counter revolutions' toward the end of the 1980s. However, it is difficult to uphold such claims by appeal to any economic facts in the history of the past twenty years.

During the two energy crises, the Soviet Union clearly subsidized the oil purchases of its allies in accordance with the price mechanism used in their mutual trade. Conversely, the price level especially of machinery exported to the Soviet Union from other Eastern bloc countries was relatively high in terms of East European price levels. No obvious financial exploitation can be shown to have occurred. Even if the price charged for energy in CMEA trade went up substantially after 1973, it did not rise as steeply as the prices on the international market could have justified.

Rather, we could say that during the past few decades, the countries of Eastern Europe, including the Soviet Union, suffered losses in welfare because the centrally planned system had failed to find the means of allocating economic resources rationally in what should have been a developed industrial society. The mechanisms of central planning had become obsolete, both internally and externally, in a situation where the basic industrial revolution had already been carried out in theory at least. A system which ignores efficiency and economic use of resources has never had much likelihood of survival.

It can, therefore, be asserted, that central planning in Europe drifted to its end despite Soviet economic support and not because of Soviet exploitation of these small economies. By the end of the 1980s, the Soviet Union had run out of the means of continuing its previous level of support.

Now, when a certain form of nostalgia about the 'good old days' has become apparent in TEs, and as neo-communist movements gather more and more support, it is worth remembering that the planned economy hardly existed anywhere in its pure form. The official economy was supplemented by a shadow economy without which the system as a whole would have been unable to function.

The Soviet shadow economy is described in the 'Shatalin Plan' in detail:

> At the present time [the late 1980s] the increased scale of the shadow economy is giving rise to public protests and numerous demands for an end to it and for an end to its influence on the authorities and other public institutions in connection with the deterioration in the country's economic position. Many people link the burgeoning of

illegal shadow economic activity with the transition to the market here.

Yet it is precisely the other way about. The shadow economy is an essential complement to the administrative-command system. The more mechanisms of the distribution of commodities substitute for normal trade then, the wider the field of activity for the shadow economy. Transition to the market is the most efficient way of eliminating it...

The **structure** of the shadow economy:

The criminal economy - economic crime (embezzlement, mercenary crimes of office and managerial crime); underground economic activity completely concealed from all forms of control (the narcotics trade, gambling, prostitution; common criminal offences against citizens' personal property as a form of the extra-economic redistribution of income (larceny, robbery with violence, theft of personal property, racketeering).

The fictitious economy - the official economy producing fictitious results reflected in the current system of accounting and accountability as real results.

The informal economy - a system of informal interactions between economic subjects based on personal relationships and direct contacts between them and complementing or substituting for the officially established procedure of the organization and realization of economic relations.

The non-legalized second economy encompasses types of individual and cooperative activity which are concealed from control, that is, are either prohibited by law or have not been registered in the established procedure or are reflected in accounts to less than the full extent.

Proceedings are instituted annually against 12.4-1.6 million persons for having committed mercenary administrative offences, including 780,00-800,000 for petty larceny, against 550,000 for the unlawful use of motor vehicles and mechanisms, and against 45,000-46,500 for illegal involvement in individual-labour activity.

Estimates of other phenomena of the shadow economy:

- artificial shortages, R40 billion (All-Union Research Institute for the Study of Consumer Demand and Trading Conditions), concealment of goods from open sale, R^ billion (USSR MVD VNII);
- cheating of customers, R10.7billion (USSR State Committee for Statistics), R4.4-R9.8 billion (USSR MVD VNII);
- in services as a whole, R14-R16 billion (USSR Gosplan Research Economics Institute);
- illegal price rises, R1.2-R1.5 billion (USSR State Committee for Prices);
- automobile profiteering, R5.7 billion, spares in automobile service, R1 billion, and income from profiteering in nonfood commodities, R1.3 billion, and alcoholic beverages, R100 million (USSR State Committee for Statistics);
- embezzlement of state and public property, R3.1 billion, petty larceny, R1.8 billion (USSR State Committee for Statistics)
- moonshining, R23 billion, including sales, R9 billion (USSR State Committee for Statistics);

- co-operators' bribes to officials, R1 billion, from individuals at the time of the acquisition, exchange and alienation of accommodations, garages, and garden plots and also their provision with amenities, R1 billion (USSR State Committee for Statistics);
- prostitution, R700 million, narcotics trade, R300 million (USSR State Committee for Statistics.

Unearned wage an unmerited bonuses for fictitious work (losses, figure padding, manufacture of substandard output), R30-R35 billion (USSR MVD VNII).

Communist societies had a 'mixed economy' of a unique type. For managers of macro- and micro-economies it is quite difficult to accept the fact that a relatively well-balanced monetary economy is necessary before the market can function freely and openly. In the old system, as pointed out by Shatalin and his team, fixed prices and shortages were twin brothers. This situation was mercilessly used by political and economic elites to the detriment of the rest of the population.

Privatization should be an urgent priority in all TEs. The objectives commonly invoked for privatization are the improvement of productive capacities and allocation of resources. In TEs there is the need to reduce the power of the existing managers of state-owned assets. The second main objective of privatization is to help to consolidate democracy by establishing a critical minimum level of private property as soon as possible.

According to the European Bank [10], in most TEs there is, unfortunately, no provision for proper enterprise control when the privatisation plans are drawn up. The lack of good corporate governance in some countries means that, although there has been considerable privatisation, the newly privatised enterprises often have only a mutant private-ownership system. Control is based on the sizeable ownership and political power of insiders in the newly privatised enterprises rather than on control by outside owners and creditors. In some TEs there is corruption in the public sector and an alarming growth of crime in the private sector. The phenomena of bribe-seeking and protection rackets are side-effects of introducing capitalism into an area of economic under-development. The new entrepreneurs, people with access to investible funds and insight into profitable investment opportunities, are the natural prey of those less favourably situated who now see the chance to enjoy conspicuous consumption of any large payoffs they can extract.

According to press reports, the steep rise in some cities of extortion rings making demands for cash payments or a share in businesses, and the accompanying rise in homicide and violence, is now a blight on existing private businesses and is scaring many entrepreneurs away from starting up new businesses. In addition to this, organised crime has recently become more professional as techniques of embezzlement and bank fraud have developed.[11]

There is a conviction in Western economics that monopoly is an enemy of efficiency and dynamism. The

---

[10] *EBRD Economic Review: Annual Economic Outlook*, September 1993 p.8-11

[11] *Newsweek*, December 13, 1993.

diversity of visions and the associated feedback processes are an enormously important benefit of market capitalism. Competition is a spur to progress since the prospect of a better product or cheaper production method will not just increase profit earned on the existing market share, but may permit the capture of a larger market share from the other enterprises. This gives extra impetus to innovation.

Therefore, it is of utmost importance that TEs introduce competition in their emerging markets, and do not replace state-owned monopolies with private ones. Only with competition can TEs achieve the economic dynamism needed to increase living-standards.

In the opinion of many Western observers, it is not necessary to worry too much about demonopolising TEs because liberalized foreign trade will immediately create the competition necessary for restructuring monopolistic industries. If TEs could only integrate themselves into the global economy, everything else would be taken care of by market forces. At the same time, it is assumed that extensive price controls will impede the development of markets and competition. In this respect the most compelling argument against price controls comes from Lipton and Sachs who point out that a transitory period of monopoly prices can promote competition by attracting entry into the private sector. If monopolies are subject to price controls, the proper price signals will be absent. The use of regulation to prevent monopolies from charging excessive prices not only fails to create competition, but may actually prevent competition from developing and thus perpetuate the structural conditions that give rise to monopoly power [12]

The problem in this context is that there are very few imports. The communist rulers left behind uncompetitive industries which, although able to serve clients within the Eastern bloc (CMEA), were hardly of use in the West. Therefore, export success, which is necessary to pay for imports, cannot come immediately after the collapse of the old system. As TEs have difficulties financing large balance of payments on current account deficits, imports must necessarily remain at a rather modest level.

Western advisers in TEs have urged host-country authorities to dismantle administrative trade barriers which were inherent in the old system. However, a totally unprotected home-market would bring serious difficulties in many branches of industry and an uncontrolled increase in unemployment.

One method of protection is the undervaluation of local currency. If the local currency is clearly undervalued, imported goods are relatively expensive and export prices are very competitive. Therefore, there is a good reason for all TEs to keep their monetary units relatively undervalued. However, this method of protectionism, as practised by TEs, has the obvious disadvantage in that it stalls the external competition which is needed to improve the efficiency of the local economy by import competition.

During the first years of transition, all TEs have been faced with the necessity of persevering with tough measures to deal with macro-economic imbalances and with

---

[12]D Lipton - J Sachs: 'Creating a Market Economy in Eastern Europe. The Case of Poland', *Brookings Papers on Economic Activity*, 1/1990, pp.75-133.

the implementation of highly complex structural reforms. A major uncertainty now is the extent to which the populations will continue to bear the heavy costs of adjustment without outright active, or even passive, opposition. There is increasing pressure to dilute or even abandon the reform process. At the same time, it is evident that without unambiguous political agreement on decision-making by consensus a credible reform programme will be extremely difficult.

Several observers have pointed out that output falls in TEs exaggerate the decline in economic welfare in so far as part of the lost production consists of goods for which there never was any demand. Even if a part of output contributes nothing to welfare, the withdrawal of its subsidy still creates the problem of re-allocating the resources employed to other purposes.

It seems to be extremely difficult to reach a broad and lasting social consensus on the steps to be taken on the stormy road to market affluence. It has become clear during the first years of transition that even if such social agreement was broadly attained initially, there is little guarantee that such a consensus could be maintained as the costs of adjustment begin to emerge.

In 1992-94 there were several signs of popular discontent which affected the political scene in TEs. The leaders of the revolutions were pushed aside. On October 25, 1992 the parliament of Lithuania decided to hold early elections, under catastrophic economic circumstances and with dramatically declining living standards. The hegemony of the Independence Movement (Sajudis) was shattered by the dramatic victory of the former Lithuanian Communist Party, renamed the Lithuanian Democratic Labour Party

(LDLP), whose chairman, Algirdas Brazauskas, was elected president.

Before that, in June 1992, in the former Czechoslovakia the left came second in elections in both the Czech and Slovak republics. The Czech and Slovak electorates decisively turned their backs on Vaclav Havel's Civic Forum. The split of the country became a fact in 1993.

In Russia, the architect of shock therapy, Yegor Gaidar, was ousted from the government after less than a year in office. His come-back to politics in the autumn of 1993 was supposed to be crowned with a sweeping electoral victory in December 1993. He and his party, the Russian Choice, suffered a humiliating defeat while the neo-fascist Liberal Democrat leader, V Zhininovsky, celebrated a considerable victory and neo-communist candidates did surprisingly well.

The most striking 'success story' of post-communism was the Balcerowicz Plan which was carried out in 1990. Yet in the September 1993 elections the Polish ex-communist Alliance of the Democratic Left (SLD) increased its vote from 12 per cent to 20.4 per cent and joined forces with the second-place Peasant Party (PSL) to form a government.

In December 1993, the Party of Democratic Socialism, the former East German Communist Party, won over 20 per cent of the vote in the East German state of Brandenburg, while the Christian Democratic Union (CDU), the Party of Chancellor Kohl, suffered a humiliating defeat. This victory symbolises the daily struggle of millions of East Germans against the hardships caused by the transition.

In May 1994, Hungary had the second free election in its reent history. What happened in these elections was a surprise for many Western observers: the Hungarian ex-communist Socialist Party (MSZP) had a landslide victory, taking more than half of all parliamentary seats.

By and large, the centre-right politicians who were the heroes of the velvet revolutions have been voted out across the TEs. At the same time, the Populist parties, both on the left and on the right, have gained a clear upper hand. This is a general tendency which can be observed in the post-communist countries; however, in the Czech Republic the reform-minded government of prime minister V Klaus has remained extremely popular.

One obvious reason for the failure of centre-right politicians has been the fact that they have been unable to find a language for addressing long-term issues such as: restructuring heavy industry; reforming the social security system, health and education, and unemployment; regulating the grey economy; and ending corruption and tackling crime. In addition, the anti-communist rhetoric on which rested much of their appeal has lost the scare value it had two years ago. Moreover, they underlined the importance of painful shock therapy solutions for the first stage of the reform and offered no alternatives or room for manoeuvre.

At the same time, it is important to realize that the new left-wing (ex communist) parties are less ideological than their forerunners and look for pragmatic solutions. The main message in their rhetoric is that the market reform must be continued, but by methods which mitigate the social shock inherent in the 'big bang' theory. There is an obvious tendency towards gradualism from the original shock therapy approach.

In this context there is a series of key issues: e.g how and by what methods the privatisation takes place; how the anchoring of property rights advances; the reshaping of the banking system, etc. Not all of these important issues can be discussed here in detail. The next chapter discusses macro-economic stabilization which is essential for a well-functioning market economy, and investments which must be the engine of restructuring. Economic stability is carefully monitored by potential foreign investors.

CHAPTER TWO

The Key Issues: Macro-Economic Stability and Investments for Restructuring

2.1 Macro-economic Stability

The heart of any market economy is the co-ordination of economic decisions via a price mechanism based on the free play of supply and demand; while the main problem of the planned economy was the shortage maintained by fixed and distorted prices. It is evident, therefore, that an early price liberalization is a *sine quo non* for the systemic change.

Price liberalization after decades of central distortions provokes two main concerns. The first is how prices will behave in an environment of monopolistic structures inherited from the communist era. The second is the concern that liberalized prices may set off uncontrollable inflation.

The transformation experience shows clearly how important it is to stabilize the economy after the initial shock of price liberalization. It was entirely predictable that TEs experienced a strong inflationary wave at the beginning of the systemic change: in the centrally-planned economies there was a phenomenon of 'hidden inflation' or a problem of 'monetary overhang' derived from the fact that money supply exceeded the supply of goods.

Once prices were freed, the most obvious shortages were supposed to be eliminated. Spending patterns started to move away from the 'forced substitution' and 'quantity-rationing' towards the sovereignty of the consumer, but limited by the purchasing power of the populace. Inflation was supposed to abate when the 'monetary overhang' was spent or eaten up by the rapid speed of inflation.

However, macro-economic stability in TEs is not only the historical 'stock problem' of the communist monetary overhang. It is also a 'flow problem': stability requires a balancing of public sector finances and the introduction of measures to control the growth in the money supply. The objective should be to ensure a tight macro-economic stance.

In fiscal policy the simple aim should be the reduction of the budget deficit coupled with moves to finance any eventual remaining deficit by selling government bonds and/or treasury bills (and not by simply printing new money in the communist manner).

The shift to a market economy will also force radical changes in the role of money and credit. Money will now have to perform an active role in guiding the allocation of resources instead of the mostly passive role it played in the period of central planning. An effective monetary policy will be a key tool in ensuring an adequate supply of money and credit, maintaining a relative stability of price level, and thus also the exchange rate of the local currency.

During the first years of post-communism, clear differences in stabilization among TEs have started to emerge.

Poland, Hungary and the former Czechoslovakia have made the greatest progress in structural reform and macroeconomic stabilization; while Bulgaria and Romania, as well as many of the former Soviet republics are lagging behind.

The price level in most of the former Soviet Union jumped sharply in January 1992 as a result of price deregulation, although this did not affect all prices. In contrast to the experience in Central Eastern Europe, however, inflation fell only temporarily during mid-1992, and then rose sharply to rates of about 20 per cent a month, or in excess of 1000 per cent a year. In Russia inflation soared in the last quarter of the year to about 25 per cent a month, raising fears of real hyperinflation. There has been a remarkable capital flight as the value of the Rouble has declined rapidly, from some 130 to the US Dollar in mid-1992 to over 1000 to the dollar in late 1993.

A major factor behind the inflationary pressure has been the excessive credit expansion by the central banks to state enterprises. In addition, the Central Bank of Russia has expanded credits to other central banks in the Rouble area on a large scale, even although such credits were in principle to have been limited after July 1992. Other factors include the explosion of inter-enterprise arrears and chaotic monetary relations in the Rouble zone. The Rouble zone finally broke up in 1993, thus allowing each country of the former USSR to pursue its own monetary policy.

It is not possible to cover all details of various stabilization policies in the former Soviet republics here. Only two short examples are given; the success of Estonia and the complete failure of the Ukraine.

Estonia, the smallest of the former Soviet republics with a population of 1.5 million, introduced its own currency the Kroon, as part of a stabilization programme in mid-1992 and pegged it to the German D-Mark. This allowed Estonia to isolate itself from the economic chaos and inflation plaguing the Rouble zone.

Fully backed by hard currency and gold reserves and linked to the D-Mark, the Kroon has emerged as one of the TEs most stable monetary units. Inflation, which in 1992 had reached some 1000 per cent, was brought down to around 20 per cent in 1993. The tough economic policies pursued by the Estonian authorities has caused severe a drop in industrial production and high unemployment. However a new comprehensive privatisation scheme elaborated in 1993, and the establishment of thousands of new enterprises operating with foreign capital, means that there is a realistic possibility of an economic growth period as early as 1994-95.

A banking crisis at the end of 1992, which affected three of Estonia's largest banks and hundreds of depositors, solicited a hardline response from the economic policy-makers to ensure that there would be no repeat. This commitment to sound money principles has encouraged a phenomenal growth of small business activity in which local individuals and foreign investors participate.

Ukraine, the second largest former Soviet republic with a population of 52 million, generated a real nightmare economy during the first two years of the post-Soviet era. In January 1992, Ukraine introduced its own interim currency, Karbovanets. In November of the same year this interim coupon became the sole legal tender, which meant that Ukraine thus withdrew from the Rouble zone.

Since then the production of these coupons has increased rapidly, while the Ukrainian GDP has dropped 20 per cent a year. In the absence of any major structural reforms, the country entered a hyperinflation trap with an inflation rate of 70-90 per cent a month by late 1993. The old planning system was partly reconstructed, with fixed prices for a series of 'strategic products'. Banks were banned from currency trading and the Kiev currency market was closed down. Enterprises were forced to sell 50 per cent of their currency holdings (including the Rouble) to the government, which was unable to service the external debt. A fixed exchange rate of some 6,000 coupons per dollar was determined for these transactions, while the blackmarket rate was 25,000 coupons per dollar. By this means, the currency holdings of enterprises were virtually confiscated.

Between September 1991 and March 1992, all the states of the former Soviet Union (FSU) became members of the International Monetary Fund (IMF), which is now trying to impose macro-economic stability in all TEs (Romania, Poland and Hungary joined the IMF before the collapse of communism).

It is a well known fact that standby credits given by the IMF - which are directed at giving short term help to countries with balance of payment problems - are always conditional. Economic policy advice given by the IMF must be carefully taken into consideration, otherwise credits are not forthcoming. Agreements between the IMF and client governments have, furthermore, a broader importance: a country in disagreement with the IMF is normally not eligible for World Bank credits; other external credits are in this case extremely difficult to acquire. This means, in effect, that the IMF determines the creditworthiness of each TE. This international organization plays a very decisive role in the TEs.

The main rule set by the IMF for TEs is linked with fiscal policy: the budget deficit in each of the TEs is not supposed to exceed 5 per cent of the GNP of the client country. Deviations from this rule seem most unlikely to be accepted. Poland, for example, has struggled for some years to balance her budget sufficiently to please IMF advisers, who show very little flexibility in the point mentioned above.

The role of the IMF in transforming the post-communist economies has been controversial during the entire post-communist era. Opponents of the IMF's hard stand argue that withholding credits gravely weakens the chances for successful stabilization. Supporters of IMF policy maintain that authorities in the client states must show a willingness to stabilize before outside financial help is forthcoming. If the conditionality mentioned above is relaxed, there is the obvious danger that money poured in will be swallowed by the notorious 'black hole' without any tangible results from the point of view of stabilization.

Senior Russian official Grigori Arbatov, director for the past twenty five years of the USA-Canada Institute in Moscow, has warned that the International Monetary Fund's 'shock therapy' policies in Russia are producing a 'very dangerous' threat to world security. Speaking on October 12 1993, at a conference on global strategic questions sponsored by the Evangelical Academy in Tutzing, Germany, Arbatov said that 'shock therapy' was devised by high-level American policy circles to 'de-industrialise' and 'destabilize' his country, to 'bring Russia to her knees'.

He claimed that the Russian population's growing awareness of this is leading to an 'anti-Western backlash' at a volatile moment with the country under 'civil war' conditions. The West, he asserted, should be 'extremely cautious' in its dealings with a nuclear power like Russia under such circumstances and should drop 'shock therapy'.

Arbatov discarded the relatively mild written speech he had submitted to the Tutzing event and stated that 'the main questions facing Russia are economic', and that 'the major mistake' made by Boris Yeltsin and others, after the failed August 1991 *putsch,* was to have supported 'shock therapy' reforms. 'Now, two years later, after the dramatic recent events of the late September-early October period, Russia is experiencing "extremely worrying problems"... 'We now have a great victory of totalitarianism, the events of the last weeks show this... The economic and social problems can become even more extreme than in the 1991-92 period. This is mainly attributable to the application of "shock therapy", the results of which are very poor'.

This citation merely serves to highlight the necessity of developing successful stabilization policies in the TEs. If the vital first transformation shock brings about a prolonged inflationary period, the foundation for the new system cannot be solid.

As mentioned above, successful macro-economic stabilization has been carried out in several previous CMEA countries, and also in Estonia which is a former Soviet republic. It is essential that authorities at the national level have the will and ability to deal with economic policy problems. It has been pointed out above that this was certainly not the case in Ukraine.

It is also useful to bear in mind that the last months of Soviet power were catastrophic from the economic point of view. In the summer of 1990, Prime Minister Ryzhkov was replaced by Valentin Pavlov who formed a government in which the hand of conservatives was greatly strengthened. Gorbachev received approval from the Supreme Soviet to accelerate reform by taking the initiative through presidential decrees. The new government put up a brave pretence that it would really go ahead with reform; indeed, it issued numerous decrees, passed laws, formed a property agency to carry out privatization, raised consumer goods prices in April 1991, among other things.

But in effect, the rightward turn at the end of summer 1990 marked the end of focused and sustained push for reform. The period from October 1990 until the coup at the end of August 1991 was wasted in a slow shuffle of pretence, reaction, incompetence and misguided policies. The year marked a slide into economic chaos. The central disaster was the failure of the supposed understanding reached at the end of 1990 concerning the split of tax revenue between the all-Union and the republican budgets both of which were in deficit.

These deficits were covered by printing money, and the monetary overhang ballooned. The only effort to deal with the overhang, already serious enough, was Pavlov's currency conversion in 1991 which resulted in virtually no decrease in the amount of money outstanding, but caused tremendous dissatisfaction and loss of confidence.[13]

[13]A controversial event in January 1991 was the monetary reform, during which large-denomination Rouble notes were withdrawn from circulation. Holders of the bills were compensated above a specified limit only if they could document the source of their resources. The reform was originally conceived as a response to counterfeiting, with subsequently

Output fell in 1991 in all sectors. In a situation where prices were controlled in varying degrees, the rapid growth in the money supply meant repressed inflation, disappearance of goods from normal channels, and disparities between blackmarket and official prices. When the government could not longer hold the line on prices, open inflation took off. Excess demand inevitably spilled over into the foreign balance. Falling output hit the USSR's major export (oil). In response the government greatly increased foreign borrowing and its a foreign debt burden the interest rates and repayments of which it could not serve based on its hard currency earnings. To cope with the problem, the USSR had to deplete its gold reserves. Investment fell, and though many of the abandoned projects were no loss, in some sectors - most importantly, the energy sector - the investment crunch planted the seeds of a further decline in output.[14]

Undoubtedly, the last years of communism left a heavy legacy for post-communist rulers, and only two options: either to recreate stability in TEs with austerity measures; or to suffer economic chaos in the form of a prolonged inflationary period. The latter can be called the 'Latin-Americanization' of the region.

stated objectives of extracting financial resources earned from illegal activities and the effective elimination of cash Rouble holdings by banks and individuals abroad. The reform retired around 4 million Roubles from currency in circulation - just under 3 per cent. The reform also led to a shift from cash/liquid assets into bank deposits.

The April 2 retail price reform increased administered prices by an average of around 80 per cent, and contributed to a 58 per cent rise in the consumer price index during the second quarter of 1991.

[14]R Campbell, 'Economic Reform in the USSR and Its Succesor States' in S Islam and M Mandelbaum (eds), *Making Markets*, Council of Foreign Relations Press, New York, 1993, pp.116-117.

The economic consequences of prolonged inflation are well known. There is a strong disincentive for savings; investment calculations are difficult; capital flight is highly likely; speculators are favoured; the low-income strata of society normally have to bear the burden; and so forth. There is also the risk that confidence in money will be entirely destroyed and that society will go back to a primitive barter economy which makes the rationality inherent in modern post-industrial society completely impossible.

It is self-evident that economic instability creates and fosters social insecurity and political populism. Therefore, it is important that economic instability is overcome in all TEs and not only in some of them. Stable development can only be achieved by the interaction of national and international economic policy making. During the first years of post-communism, both positive and negative cases have come into being in the former CMEA region.

2.2 Saving and Investment

One of the greatest dramas of economic history took place in the late 1920s and early 1930s when the 'shock therapy' of Soviet planning began. Based on the Stalinist slogan of 'building up socialism in one country, this 'big bang' of central planning converted the whole country into a huge building site almost overnight.

The burden of domestic investment at the beginning of central planning fell exclusively on domestic savings. (Before World War I a significant contribution had come from foreign capital). How was the vast investment plan of the early planning period financed? In part by the sales of bonds, which had become almost compulsory by this time - a recalcitrant citizen who failed to volunteer to buy bonds might well suffer undesirable consequences. And then there was the printing press. The money supply rose dramaticallly.[15]

Over-investment and monetary financing of them became a communist obsession. Investments throughout the communist bloc took a consistently high share of the GNP. Monetary equilibrium never played a decisive role in the communist capital formation; if there were not enough savings available for the investment boom, more money was printed. At the same time, efficiency criteria were shaky or missing altogether. The result was a large-scale waste of scarce resources.

In Western economics one of the most important basic rules is that savings are supposed to be equal to investments. If there is a shortage of local savings but good investment opportunities, foreign capital can be brought in to bridge the gap.

It is paradoxical that, after decades of fierce capital formation in centrally planned economies, there is now a huge need for investments. There are several reasons for this paradox: large scale misallocation of capital took place under communism; maintenance of capital stock was grossly neglected; and the quality of investment goods was inferior.

The East German case will serve to illustrate the magnitude of the problem involved in capital stock in the TEs. Immediately after the collapse of the Berlin Wall, it was estimated that the value of GDR's capital stock was some DEM 400 billion. This figure was very soon halved. In the autumn of 1992, the German Ministry of Finance estimated

---

[15] A Nove: *An Economic History of the USSR*, London 1990, pp 200-201.

that the productive capacities in some 8,500 enterprises with some 4 million workers in the former GDR had a total value of only DEM 81 billion.[16]. Chancellor Helmut Kohl declared that the burden of the East German communist legacy, which must be borne by the German taxpayer, is DEM 400 billion.

Naturally, the GDR is a special case. The monetary union with West Germany in July 1990 brought an abrupt end to the protection of the communist way of production. In new, competitive circumstances under which the former markets collapsed, the value of assets also fell apart totally. It was extremely hard for the officials of Treuhandanstalt, the privatization agency of the GDR's property, to organise take-overs.

Unfortunately, not all of the TEs have rich neighbours willing to pick up the bill of post-communist renewal. Basically, the investment injection needed to renovate TE capacities must be financed by local savings. With low living standards and decreased incomes, the propensity to save can be supposed to be relatively low. There is, however, no universal empirical evidence for the assumption made in economic theory that the propensity to save increases with income growth in the household sector. In some of the richest OECD countries (Sweden, Netherlands, USA), the propensity to save in the household sector is amazingly low (see table).

According to Professor Lester Thurow from MIT, American private corporations are world-class savers, while America's private citizens are not. Less is saved than is invested in housing (3.3 per cent versus 4.1 per cent of

[16]*Neues Deutschland,* November 11, 1992.

SAVINGS RATIOS

	Households[a]			National[b]		
	1968-73	**74-79**	**80-90**	**1968-73**	**74-79**	**80-90**
Australia	11.8	12.6	8.1	25.6	22.7	19.8
Belgium	16.1	16.9	13.8	25.1	21.6	16.7
Canada	7.5	12.4	12.8	22.2	22.6	20.1
France	14.1	15.5	14.2	27.1	24.9	20.3
Germany	13.6	13.3	12.4	27.1	22.6	22.8
Holland	14.7	13.5	3.0	27.0	23.0	22.2
Italy	19.5	22.3	17.8	28.9	25.7	21.8
Japan	18.0	21.6	15.8	38.5	32.8	31.8
Spain	10.8	10.1	6.6	26.4	23.9	20.8
Sweden	4.0	4.2	0.3	22.9	19.5	17.0
Switzerland	14.2	11.9	7.3	32.1	27.7	30.0
UK	5.1	6.4	9.5	19.8	16.8	16.6
USA	9.5	9.6	5.4	19.6	19.8	16.5
EC	13.0	14.2	11.8	25.4	22.5	20.4
OECD	11.7	13.0	10.3	24.4	22.8	20.6

[a]Net household savings as % of disposable household income

[b]Gross national savings as % of GDP

Source: OECD

GNP in 1990), and as a result individuals actually subtract from, rather than contribute to, the pool of savings available to finance output-enhancing forms of investment. Voluntary personal savings (the savings made after Americans make compulsory contributions to their pension funds) are actually negative.[17] In the 1980s the United States borrowed resources from the rest of the world to keep its consumption growing faster than its productivity - borrowing about $1,000 billion from abroad. According to Thurow, sooner or later any nation will reach the end of its borrowing capacity and have sold off the assets that foreigners wish to purchase, and its international capacity to borrow is exhausted.[18]

Professor Assar Lindbeck, an eminent Swedish economist states that Swedish household savings dwindled in the 1970s and 1980s to minus 5 per cent of the disposable income of households, compared with about plus 10 per cent in other European countries. Reduced private savings slow down the accumulation of national wealth. Moreover, entrepreneurship requires private wealth and hence private saving. In spite of high tax rates, Sweden's public-sector borrowing accounts for a heavy 13 per cent of GNP which shifts the welfare burden to future generations.[19]

Kornai argues extremely strongly against the application of the so-called 'Swedish model' in post-communist Europe:

> 'As a bitter joke has it in Budapest, we now have Hungarian wages minus Swedish taxes. Regrettably, a number of incompetent and superficial Western observers have also been taken in; they were inclined to see the new Hungarian tax system as a token of the country's "Westernization" ... I would express myself in a less

---

[17] L Thurow, *Head to Head. The Coming Economic Battle Among Japan, Europe and America*, London, 1993, pp 263-4.

[18] Ibid., p.165.

[19] *Newsweek*, December 20, 1993.

> extreme way if Hungary had a long period of capitalist development behind it, if sizeable private property were already established, if we had the incentive that comes from the knowledge that private wealth amassed by honest toil and business integrity could be inherited by children and grandchildren. In other words, I would support a measure of redistributive taxation if I were a citizen of today's France, for instance, although as a citizen of the Western world, I would still find the extreme form of redistributive taxation practised in Sweden excessive. ... The main item on the agenda is still to set the mind of every participant in the private sector at rest, reassuring the peasant smallholder, the farmer beginning to modernize, the private artisan, and the owner of a large private firm: Have no fear, go ahead and accumulate![20]

Kornai is here pointing out that a 'primitive capitalist accumulation' must take place in TEs before a Western-style welfare state can be afforded. The prime task of economic policy is supposed to be the creation of circumstances in which savings can be increased to meet the need to finance investments.

In theory, societies do not need private savings. Governments could[21], if the system were so organized, achieve surpluses in their budgets large enough to finance private investment. Governments would simply lend, rather than borrow, in the nation's capital markets. It is, however, unlikely that governments in market economies are going to have surpluses large enough to obviate the need for private savings.

---

[20] J Kornai, *The Road to a Free Economy*, New York-London, 1990, pp.204-205.

[21] Government savings are general government revenue less current expenditure. Government capital spending is classed as investment. Thus, although the budget balance is often taken as a proxy for government savings, there can be a large difference between the two.

This theoretical model is hardly applicable in TEs that are obliged to create a reasonable social safety net which should reflect the social consensus on the adjustment burden society will be willing to absorb and how equitably the burdens should be distributed. It would be utterly false to claim to be able to protect almost everyone against this burden and to keep the budget reasonably balanced at the same time. Running budget surpluses in order to advance national savings is not a feasible alternative.

In any case TEs should somehow be able to create an environment favourable to private investment and entrepreneurship. It can hardly be expected that domestic savings will suffice, especially in the short-run austerity period with its characteristic anti-inflationary economic policy in which personal savings are virtually wiped out by strong price hikes.

It is impossible to obtain systematic information on personal savings in the various TEs. Obviously household saving rates decreased throughout Eastern Europe during the early period of post-communism. This is mainly attributed to improved consumption choices: it is the inevitable correlate of the transition from a regime of forced savings (or lack of consumption opportunities) to one of market-based, decentralized savings decisions. Lately, there have been interesting reversals in that downward tendency in some TEs. In the case of Hungary, this has been linked to increased confidence in the financial system and other products of the reform, or, alternatively, to increased fear of job loss and other factors of economic uncertainty.

The banking sector in TEs has a tough time adjusting to the demands of the market. For banks the pain is twofold:

their own problems - bad debts, limited services, outdated technology - are compounded by the deep recession of post-communism. Everyday brings fresh trouble for the bank's biggest customers, undermining the ability of banks to modernize their own operations.

Banking problems are inherited from the old regimes and are the result of their policies of granting mass at low interest rates to the large state monopolies. In addition, these credits had no discernible period of maturity. Banks in TEs must now try to clean up the mess their predecessors left behind. Obviously, local governments must find ways to support the banking system and clear the balance sheets. Scarce resources must be used to restart financial institutions in the period of transition.

In the medium-term, it is of utmost importance that TEs have well-functioning money and capital markets which will be able to allocate national savings - assumed to be relatively low due to low living standards - as effectively as possible for productive purposes. At the same time, Kornai's arguments must be taken into consideration: there must be leeway for capital accumulation, even if there are extensive social needs in the period of transition. 'Social Darwinism', in which there are considerable income differentials - with the state playing a much smaller part, is needed if new prosperity is going to develop.

It is self-evident that this period of early post-communist capitalism creates huge social tensions. 'Profiteering', which was criminal under the old system, is supposed to become not only socially acceptable but to be the engine of the new beginning. At the same time, new social needs, especially unemployment benefits, are supposed to be taken into consideration under circumstances in which balancing the state budget is already extremely difficult.

According to the World Bank, the 'secret' of the Newly Industrialized Countries (NIC) in South-East Asia in their economic success is simple and understandable: these countries have reached extraordinarily high savings and investment ratios which clearly out-perform the equivalent figures in the OECD area. Among the OECD countries there are two countries with exceptionally high savings ratios, Japan and Switzerland (both over 30 per cent in the 1980s).[22]

It can be assumed that there will not be enough domestic savings in TEs to finance all the investments needed to modernise local capacities and to make them competitive. Thus, external sources of capital are certainly needed. External economic links are discussed in the next chapter.

Before going over to the next topic discussing the external economy in TEs, some concluding remarks on the present chapter are appropriate. It is absolutely vital that TEs reach reasonable price stability soon after the systemic transformation. If this objective is not reached during the first years of transition, there is a danger that social problems will be aggravated, savings will not take place and reasonable calculations about long-term investments become difficult. The popularity of economic decision-makers will necessarily decrease and populist (extremist) groups will grow stronger. There is already enough evidence that relative price stability can be achieved reasonably, even in the extremely difficult circumstances of the post-Soviet economy (Estonia for instance).

---

[22] IBRD: *The East-Asian Miracle: Economic Growth and Public Policy, Washington, 1993.*

Furthermore, a period of sustainable and stable economic growth after the transitional shock calls for capital accumulation and effective mechanisms to allocate scarce capital. If there is a 'get rich quick' mentality in TEs, it is important from the point of view of social stability that criminal elements of society will be dealt with effectively by the authorities. It is no accident that in various opinion polls throughout the TE region, people are seriously concerned with increasing crime and speculation.

If capital accumulation is allowed and encouraged by economic policy-makers, they ought to bear in mind that there are three theoretical optional uses for profits: they can be used for conspicuous consumption by capitalists who have earned them; profits can be brought out of the country, even where the need for capital in the home market is obvious; or profits can be re-invested on the spot.

It is self-evident that only the third option, which calls for the 'Protestant ethic' of new capitalists, is beneficial from the point of view of the society as a whole. A situation in which newly won entrepreneurial liberties are being used for large-scale tax evasion and profits for luxury goods and/or massive capital flight, will naturally be unbearable from the point of view of social justice. In such a situation the burden of transition is unevenly divided between various groups of the population and far-reaching popular discontent is inevitable.

It was shown above that some of the richest countries of the world, Sweden and the USA, have actually negative household savings which is amazing from the point of view of economic theory. Relatively high income does not, therefore, guarantee large bank accounts and liquidity of the financial markets.

It is however clear, on the other hand, that a population which uses some 50-60 per cent of an average family budget for foodstuffs and beverages (as in post-communist Russia) can hardly have a high propensity to save in the household sector. If the over-all living standard remains low for a long period of time, there is a danger that the economy will enter a vicious circle or a poverty trap in which investments of any reasonable magnitude cannot take place. It is quite common in that kind of society to try to overcome poverty by creating money which causes an inflationary spiral of wages and prices and results in shortages. Every TE must make the utmost effort to avoid this scenario becoming a reality.

CHAPTER THREE

The Global Economy and Post-Communism

3.1 Foreign Trade in Transition

The experience of the past four decades offers strong evidence of the close linkage between liberal trade and exchange regimes and economic prosperity. The liberalization of trade in manufactured goods among the industrial countries (OECD) was one of the principal reasons for the rapid growth of world output in the 1950s and 1960s. One of the key questions in TEs is how they can share in, and contribute to, continued gains in global economic performance.

As TEs wish to integrate themselves quickly and as fully as possible with the international economy, special attention must be devoted to the reconstruction of their trade and foreign exchange sectors. As mentioned above, openness to the world economy will help to provide a system of relative prices and much needed competition for domestic producers.

In the former economic system of central planning, there was pervasive protection against imports. This took various forms of export and import quotas, foreign exchange licensing, often through bilateral trade agreements, and other even less transparent methods.

A unique kind of 'dual protectionism' was established for the intersocialist division of labour. On the one hand, the state monopoly of each socialist country protected its own developing industries from external competition; but, on the other hand, the small CMEA countries did not have to worry about the marketing of their new industrial goods because demand from the immense Soviet market was virtually limitless. The Soviet Union paid for these goods with raw materials and energy, thus guaranteeing the supply of these products to the CMEA area.

The demise of the CMEA and the resultant collapse of its system of trade and clearing payments placed the small TEs in the unpleasant predicament of losing their supply of raw materials that were cheaper than those sold on the world market. These countries also discovered that they were structured to produce investment goods that were technologically backward and unsaleable in the Western world.

As a result, a shock wave, caused by external factors of socialist disintegration, swept through the TE region during the first years of transition. This external shock can be illustrated by the following figures.

Exports of TEs
(1989-1992, changes in percentages)

	Czecho-slovakia	Hungary	Poland	ex-USSR	Bulgaria	Romania
Total Exports	-7	6.5	23.5	-14.4	-64.3	-62.7
to OECD	40.6	56	55.7	19.8	58.1	-56.5
EC	62	87	86.1	38.9	72.4	-74.9
ex-CMEA	-50.7	-26.2	1.9	-43.9	-86.1	-64.9
ex-USSR	-54.8	-14.2	-7.8	-	-87	-62.2
Other	18	-27.9	-17	-32.8	19.3	-67.8

Source: WIIW

As the figures show, there were huge differences in the external shock of the early years of post-communism. Bulgarian exports to the ex-USSR decreased by no less than 84 per cent, while the equivalent figure in the Polish case was only about -8 per cent and in Hungary some -14 per cent. Czechoslovakia and Romania also suffered heavy losses of exports in the former Soviet market. Hungary and Poland were able to overcompensate their export losses in the ex-CMEA market by increased sales in the OECD area, especially in the EC. Czechoslovakian exports suffered a modest overall setback of 7 per cent, while Bulgarian and Romanian exports dropped by over 60 per cent overall.

At the beginning of the post-communist era, the TEs were minor players in the global economy. This can be illustrated by some simple figures

The Economic Relevance of External Trade for Selected Countries and Areas (1990)

	Czechoslovakia	Hungary	Poland	EC	EFTA
Exports (US$ Bn)	11.7	9.1	16.2	13652	224
Exports GNP(%)	28.1	40.0	25.0	21.6	26.0
Exports per capita (US$)	745	858	426	3959	6871

Source: World Bank

In Hungary, where exports make up 40 per cent of GNP, exports per capita are only a bit more than one fifth of the equivalent figure in the EC. In EFTA, exports per capita are nine times higher than in the former Czechoslovakia and sixteen times higher than in Poland. These differences are striking.

For the West, the Eastern market plays a minor role only. TEs import no more than some $70 billion yearly from OECD countries. The East (TEs) have a share of less than 3 per cent in the overall Western (OECD) exports and imports. These extremely low figures ought to be borne in mind when East-West trade is discussed in the post-communist era: obviously, the fate of economic reforms in Eastern Europe will depend on how successful the reforming countries will become in penetrating Western markets. This success can hardly cause disturbances in the West because of the marginal importance of Eastern trade to OECD economies.

From the point of view of TEs, it is essential that they gain reasonable access to Western markets and, at the same time, are able somehow to protect their own industries during the process of transition. It is understandable that the old methods of administrative foreign trade control have been dismantled and replaced by conventional commercial policy instruments, mainly tariffs and exchange rate policies. It is impossible here to describe all the details of this systemic change in every TE, each with different foreign trade mechanisms. Only some general features of post-communist exchange-rate policies can be discussed here.

In the old system of central planning, official exchange rates (ERs) were artificially fixed at unrealistic levels. There was also a plethora of other quasi-official rates for certain transactions. With the systemic change, trade liberalization and the introduction of internal convertibility with the unification of the ERs have taken place.

At the beginning of the transitional period, TE officials were confronted with two important issues when they started to make their currencies internally convertible: they had to define the level of the ER and the regime of ER. No fixed rules prevail in this context.

There has been a tendency in TEs to select an excessively devalued exchange rate at the beginning of the systemic change. This strategy has the obvious advantage that it makes exports extremely competitive and imports expensive; which is sensible from the balance of trade point of view. The undervaluation of local currency is one important factor behind the quick geographic restructuring of foreign trade in TEs: exports to the West became very competitive pricewise via ER policy.

Obviously, devalued original ERs also contributed to inflation on the home market during the first years of transition. As an additional disadvantage of an undervalued ER, one can report the cementing of local industrial structures. As the ER clearly protects local industries from Western competition by keeping imports artificially expensive, the economically rational restructuring of outdated capacities will be prolonged.

According to the Vienna Institute for Comparative Economic Studies [23], there has been an appreciation of the real effective ER in Poland, Hungary and Czechoslovakia (Czech Republic since 1993) in the early 1990s. This means that inflation on the home market has not been compensated for by nominal devaluations (price increases outstripped devaluations). In Hungary and the Czech Republic local money is begged to a basket of currencies. Poland has a 'crawling beg' ER regime which means that local zloty is devalued by some 2 per cent each month.

Bulgaria has opted for a floating ER, while Romania has a managed float with some elements of currency rationing. The Romanian case seems to be a nightmare scenario: economic reforms in tatters and inflation running to some 15 per cent a month (in 1993); the official ER has depreciated rapidly, but not rapidly enough (due to Central Bank interventions) to reflect the local inflation. Thus a black market for hard currency, as in the communist era, has returned: the price of a dollar in the black market is about double the official ER for the Romanian Lei.

In the former Soviet Union, the restructuring of the monetary sphere has been extremely complicated. The Central Bank (Gosbank) was replaced at the end of 1991 by a decentralized banking system in which the main branch of Gosbank in each of the former republics was transformed into a more or less independent central bank.

---

[23](WIIW, Mitgliederinformaton 1993/11)

The Central Bank of Russia had the sole power to issue rouble currency. Nevertheless, the other central banks could extend credit to their governments and to domestic enterprises by creating bank reserves, drawing on credit lines at the Central Bank of Russia, and in many cases issuing coupons (local money).

Thus, there were no proper arrangements in 1992 to control monetary expansion in the rouble zone. In an attempt to regain control, the Central Bank of Russia centralized the processing of interstate payments in its Moscow branch and introduced restrictions on payment orders, although doing so further disrupted interstate trade. Inflationary pressures in the rouble zone were reinforced when, in the second half of 1992, the Central Bank of Russia itself reversed its policy of restrained domestic credit expansion in order to meet the growing financing requirements of the government.

In the winter of 1992-93, the shortage of currency and the blockage of the inter-republican settlement system led to a *de facto* dissolution of the rouble zone. Rouble deposits earned in one state could not be used to make payments in other states. In the summer of 1993, Russia carried out the withdrawal of old banknotes to the republics. Following this ultimatum, the former Soviet republics faced a dilemma: either to agree to the monopoly of the Central Bank of Russia and to forget about their own independence in monetary matters, or like the Baltic States to try to obtain financial sovereignty.[24]

In the meantime, the rouble in Moscow continues to float, as it has done since the demise of the USSR. At the

---

24 (See Tiusanen, *The Baltic States: Small Countries in Transition*, Helsinki 1993, EVA.)

beginning of 1994, Russia banned the use of Western currencies in its internal payments.

One of the most important economic issues of post-communism in the next few years is how to maintain viable trade links in the framework of the former Soviet republics. This question comprises not only the system of payments but also that of prices. The non-Russian republics now face world market prices in their inter-republican trade. This basically means a rapidly increasing energy bill for several former Soviet republics which have limited local sources of energy (e.g Ukraine, Moldova and Georgia).

Foreign trade problems in TEs are therefore not only limited to questions of reshaping East-West trade in the post-communist period, but also relate to the revitalisation of trade relations within the TEs. Viable solutions must be found if the process of transition in the former non-Russian Soviet republics is to run smoothly. Very little attention has been paid by the West to the negative and potentially explosive economic consequences of the disintegration of the Soviet empire.

Certain generalized conclusions can be drawn from points made in this section. Some TEs (Poland, Hungary and the Czech Republic) have been fairly successful in re-shaping their geographical trade patterns during the first years of post-communism. At the same time, it can be asserted that relative undervaluation of several TE currencies have made exports excessively profitable (in relation to the domestic market), which has contributed an outflow of resources at a time of severe domestic constraint and aggravated the domestic inflation problem.

In discussing exchange rates in TEs, the redistribution of wealth ought also to be taken into consideration. In the post-communist era, a historical privatization process, which is also open to foreign investors, has been launched. A clearly depreciated exchange rate makes acquisition of host-country (TE) assets relatively inexpensive for foreign investors (in comparison with potential buyers from within). Therefore, there is a danger that the citizens of TEs will have the impression that 'the family silver' (the best productive assets) of the East will be sold cheaply to foreigners.

At the same time, there is an urgent need to import capital for the restructuring of TEs which inherited a significant debt burden from the period of central planning. According to the IMF[25], TEs had payments of their external debt service in the range of $30bn a year in 1990-91. This means that massive loans from the West cannot be used to fund economic transition.

It is likely that, during the first years of transition, TEs will attract some portfolio-investments from the outside world; but that none of these will be substantial. Private and institutional investors can hardly assess the risks of the newly established joint stock companies or privatized units which now have shares. It takes time to organize and develop secondary markets for TE securities, which will undoubtedly be regarded as extremely risky investments for several years to come.

Therefore, it is essential for all TEs to try to attract foreign direct investments (FDIs) from the outside world. The development of FDI activity in TEs is surely one of the most interesting components of the transitional process.[26]

---

[25] *World Economic Outlook*, 1993.

[26] FDI is used in this paper to describe the activity in which risk capital from one country is directly invested in another. FDIs can take various forms: a foreign investor sets up a new wholly-owned company in the

3.2 Foreign Direct Investments and the Transition Process

All TEs are chronically short of capital. Therefore, they are hoping to attract FDIs through joint ventures (JVs), the sale of state-owned enterprises and new capital formation. Policy-makers in TEs hope that such transfers will provide not only financial resources by capital inflows, but also help TEs to gain access to modern technology and managerial skills.

The process of FDI-inflow poses several problems which have parallels in the concerns expressed about the role of transnational corporations in developing countries and the cautious approach to liberalizing capital movement in Western Europe after World II. The main problem here is the issue of property rights and whether these should be acquired by foreigners, in which case the society must be willing to accept the resulting dilution of its economic sovereignty. However, in TEs whose scope for autonomy was so restricted for so long by Soviet-type development precepts, questions of sovereignty are likely to be particularly sensitive.

A special economic problem in TEs is the possible undervaluation of the capital stock during the initial phases of the transition. A sharply depreciated exchange rate may give foreign capital the opportunity to indulge in rent-seeking or monopolistic activities which are unlikely to bring optimal economic benefits to the host country.

---

host country (greenfield investment); a foreign investor can set up a joint venture with a local partner; a foreign investor can enact an acquisition of a company existing abroad, whereby the take-over can be total or partial.

In the communist era, there were some JVs in the East in which capitalist and communist units shared the equity. Romania and Hungary had already allowed East-West JVs in their respective territories in the early 1970s. Before the collapse of communism, all European CMEA (except the German Democratic Republic) countries had accepted JVs .

Mixed marriages, however, never became popular between capitalist and communist firms. There was a series of reasons for that: the ideological, economic and legal environment in the CMEA-countries was alien to Western firms; JVs operating inside the planned economies faced serious supply problems unfamiliar to them; the CMEA market was not an integrated region in the Western sense of the term; monetary and capital markets in the JV host country were hardly comparable to those in the West; labour markets were extremely inflexible; local currencies in all CMEA countries were inconvertible which made profit repatriation not entirely impossible, but extremely difficult.

In the early 1990s the situation has radically changed. The economic environment in TEs has begun to resemble that found in market economies. Labour costs in TEs are much cheaper than those in the OECD countries. Current account convertibility of TE monetary units has been principally carried out. As repatriation of profits is part of the current account, there is an additional incentive for FDIs to take place in TEs.

Thus, it is understandable that the interest of Western investors in TEs has increased rapidly during the first years of transition. There were only a couple of hundred operating JVs in the CMEA area at the end of the communist era. According to the United Nations Commission for Europe (ECE), which monitors FDIs in TEs regularly, there were over 70,000 units registered in 1993. The development according to ECE statistics has been breath-takingly vigorous.

However, FDI registration by number in TEs gives an incomplete picture of the economic importance of FDIs. These statistics do not tell anything about activities of firms with foreign involvement (whether registered units are active or dormant) as the amount of foreign capital input is not included.

In TEs foreign investors determine the apportionment of economic values. Thus, in many FDI cases, all or part of the foreign capital stake is contributed in kind - and not in cash. It is not easy to determine how large a share of FDIs in TEs is actually in non-monetary form.

WIIW has listed those Western capital contributions which have been paid according to balance of payments statistics. These figures give some impression of the capital inflow involved in FDIs in TEs.

Western Capital Paid in (1993)
Balance of Payments Statistics, US$ bn)
cumulative total

Bulgaria	0.12
Czech Republic	2.20
Slovakia	0.30
Hungary	4.00
Poland	0.50
Romania	0.13
Russia	0.90

These figures show that only the relatively modest sum of $8 billion has been paid in cash by Western firms within the framework of FDIs in TEs. The table also shows that Hungary has been by far the most successful TE in attracting capital inflow via FDIs. The Czech Republic, which is in second place, has received only slightly more than half of the Hungarian figure. Other TEs are considerably lower.

According to the EBRD, FDIs in TEs increased rapidly in 1991 to some $2.4 billion from $0,3 billion in 1990. The equivalent figure for 1992 was $2,7 billion (see table).

FOREIGN DIRECT INVESTMENT, SELECTED RECIPIENTS (US$, millions)

	1990	1991	1992
Sub-Saharan Africa	669	1,746	1,280
South Asia	291	356	420
East Asia and Pacific	10,885	13,021	15,060
Eastern Europe	300	2,393	2,700
Latin America and Caribbean	7,725	12,766	13,778
of which			
Argentina	2,008	2,481	2,538
Brazil	236	209	261
Chile	249	576	640
Mexico	2,632	4,762	6,191
Total Developing Countries	**24,008**	**33,907**	**38,252**

Source: EBRD

In 1991-92, TEs received just over 7 per cent of FDIs enacted in developing countries. In these two years, Mexico alone has attracted more than double the amount of FDIs in comparison to Eastern Europe.

In these comparisons, it is useful to bear in mind that the majority of FDIs traditionally take place within the OECD area. Capital in direct investments moves mainly from one rich country to another; three quarters of FDIs flow inside the industrialized world. In the early 1990s the EC area has been the main recipient of FDIs, receiving some $85 billion in 1990 and some $70 billion in both 1991 and 1992.

There are very few estimates on the economic influence of foreign-owned and partly foreign-owned firms in TEs so far. The EBRD, which has the right to become involved in equity investments in TEs, has provided the figures below relating to five TEs.

Importance of Foreign-owned Companies in the Economy, mid-1992 (shares in percentages)

	Employment	Value Added	Exports
Estonia	0.6	1.8	1.3
Hungary	4.5	9.0	16
Poland	1.3		4.0
Russia	0.1-0.2	0.9	1.4
Ukraine	0.1-0.2	0.3	1.4

Source: EBRD

Hungary is the only country in the table in which FDIs have already had a substantial economic impact: foreign-owned companies account for 4.5 per cent of total employment and 9 per cent of local value added. In the sphere of exports, the equivalent figure is even higher, 16 per cent. The figures for the other TEs in the table reveal only limited input by foreign companies. There is one interesting detail in these EBRD figures: in each of the countries shown, the share of foreign-owned companies in exports is higher than in employment.

Although there has not so far been any systematic monitoring of FDIs in TEs, we can draw some conclusions from such scattered statistics as are available. It is obvious that the systemic change in Eastern Europe has caused a real explosion in FDI numbers in TEs while, at the same time, there is relatively little substance to the investments made so far. References to amounts committed on long term bases often produce a misleading picture of the real magnitude of capital inflows within the FDI framework. It is also clear that a concentration of FDIs in certain TEs is taking place. This fact leads to uneven development prospects within the TE region. Certain countries are clearly prioritized by foreign investors.

Furthermore, it can be assumed on the basis of the given data that FDIs strongly influence the export capability of TEs. Therefore, there is a very strong reason for all TEs to continue to try to attract FDIs in the future, as international competitiveness grows even more important.

There are several reasons why Western FDIs have not resulted in a mass invasion of TEs during the first years of transition. The 'investment climate' in TEs is clearly not ideal because, among other flaws: TE markets are not integrated and are not wealthy; there is a general political and economic instability; the legal and contractual environment is in many senses unclear; the local infrastructure is not on the Western level; and regional trade-policy arrangements are far from perfect.

The recession in the West is obviously another of the reasons why there has been a reluctance to invest abroad and at home. The post-communist economic slump, which is dealt with in the next chapter, has unquestionably had a negative effect on FDIs in TEs also.

3.3 Examples of Business Activities in TEs

The car is said to be the trademark of capitalism, symbolizing personal freedom and wealth. The Trabant, the small car made in East Germany, was the symbol of communism; it made plenty of noise with very little substance in it.

In the communist era, there was co-operation between Eastern and Western car manufacturers. The Soviet-built Lada was a result of a licence agreement with Italian Fiat. The Romanian-built Dacia was produced under the Renault licence. Many East European party bosses preferred to drive a Mercedes, to show that one was more equal than the other. However, it was not possible for the East German party elite to order Mercedes, which was a symbol of West German industrial success, and so they drove Volvos. As a result, the district of East Berlin where the 'big-wigs' lived, was called 'Volvograd'.

After the collapse of communism, car-makers from OECD countries began to make negotiate contracts within the TEs. One of the most sensational contracts in this sphere was when German Volkswagen bought a 31 per cent stake in Skoda (Czechoslovakia) for DM620 million in 1991 and pledged to invest some DM7 billion by the year

2000 for modernisation. It was agreed to boost VW's holding to 70 per cent.

In the autumn of 1993, Volkswagen cancelled a major investment package for Skoda. Consternation and anger greeted the move to pull out of the DM1.4 billion plan hours before it was due to be signed in London. In a bland statement, issued by VW, it was said that enhanced productivity levels meant that its planned investment programme could be sharply scaled down.

The Skoda package had been negotiated with the European Bank for Reconstruction and Development and an international banking consortium led by the Dresdner Bank. Officially, neither would comment on developments, but privately banking circles made it clear that the institutions involved were seething.[27]

According to the *Financial Times*[28], relations between the Czech government and the German car maker had soured following a dispute caused by Skoda's decision to increase the prices of its cars substantially, and Czech concerns that VW was no longer interested in developing a local network of suppliers.

Fiat, the Italian car maker, assumed full operating control in FSN, the Polish car factory, after lengthy negotiations which were finalised late in 1993. This agreement, in which Fiat's commitment is about $2 billion, is the biggest in the Polish privatization process.

The former FSN, which has been renamed Fiat Auto Poland, is Fiat's sole production location in the world for its smallest cars; the outdated 126, which is sold only in

---

[27] *The European*, September 23-26, 1993.
[28] *Financial Times*, September 24, 1993.

Poland, and the Cinquecento, which was launched for sale throughout Europe in 1991.

Fiat's long-term links with Poland, with local production presence, has allowed it to greatly increase its share of the Polish market for imported cars. According to Fiat's estimate, it accounted for around 55 per cent of all new car sales in 1993, compared with 39 per cent in 1992. At the beginning of 1994, Fiat will expand its operations in Poland with the local assembly of its Uno small car set [29]

Jaguar is moving into the markets of the former Soviet Union with a sales push that will help make it a global luxury car supplier. The British based firm, owned by Ford, is developing a sales network in St Petersburg and Moscow through its Finnish importer and is also moving into the Ukraine, the Baltic states and Azerbaijan.

Like Rolls Royce motors, which in 1993 opened a showroom in Moscow, Jaguar is capitalising on the developing market for Western luxury products which are keenly sought by the new class of millionaires. Jaguar is already advancing in Poland where sales of about 40 cars a year are expected, and to the Czech Republic where annual sales could amount to 20 cars. Jaguar sells around 28,000-29,000 cars each year.[30]

The Boeing company announced the opening of its research centre in Moscow in 1993. The centre will co-ordinate Boeing's research and technological projects in Russia and may become the launching pad for the US company's broad offensive in Russia.

Russia's leading researchers have been facing problems in financing their projects and the creation of the new cen-

---

[29] *Financial Times*, November 2, 1993.
[30] *The Times*, October 24, 1993.

tre will allow them to proceed with their research. The centre intends to analyze what Boeing's plans have in common with Russia's aerospace researchers in order to decide which joint projects should be developed and which Russian specialists should be engaged in long-term research.

Some twenty Russian specialists work with the centre under contracts with Russian institutes and universities. Their salaries are the same as those paid in the US. The centre is engaged in mathematical modelling for aerodynamic research on the designing of aircraft, research into the application of new materials, and the study of the impact of low temperatures on aircraft fuel systems[31]

Hyundai, South Korea's largest business group, plans to produce passenger aircraft using Russian technology. In 1993 Hyundai Precision & Industry, which manufactures railway and other transport equipment established a joint venture (JV) with Yakovlev of Russia in which the Koreans have a 51 per cent stake. The Russian partner will be responsible for the design and development of the passenger aircraft based on 150-seat Yak 42H and the 30-seat Yak 40H. They will be assembled by Hyundai in South Korea.

Hyundai will also establish a global marketing and after-sales network for both the Korean-made airliners and other aircraft produced by Yakovlev. The Korean government wants the country to become one of the world's ten leading aerospace producers by the year 2020 and has budgeted some WON250 billion (£209 million) for the development of a medium-sized passenger aircraft[32].

---

[31] *Commersant,* September 15 1993.
[32] *Financial Times,* November 9, 1993.

The Russians also have a tradition in making light aircraft. New models have been developed by Aviatika, a firm established by the Moscow aircraft-building association, the Moscow Aviation Institute and the Zhukovsky-based test flying institute. The firm has sold more than 100 Aviatika plans over the first eighteen months of its existence to private individuals; in Italy, Spain, Hungary, Brazil, the United States and Australia. According to *Commersant,*[33] the planes are incredibly cheap, at $16,000-24,000 and attract more demand than the production unit can meet.

It is certainly not an overstatement to say that McDonalds is one of the best known companies in the world. Altogether the US company has some 14,000 restaurants with operations in almost seventy countries.

With communism nothing was fast and food was normally in short supply. Therefore, it was bound to be a sensation when McDonalds came to Moscow during the last years of Soviet power and started serving fast food.

In 1988, McDonalds Canada established a JV with Moscow City in which the Western partner has a 49 per cent stake. In 1993 it was announced that a total of $70 million had been invested in the Moskva-McDonalds venture; comprising a food-processing unit in Solntsevo (near Moscow), a restaurant in Pushkin Square, a thirteen-storey building in Oganyova Street (with a two storey restaurant) and one more restaurant on the old Arbat. By the summer of 1993 all three restaurants were in operation.

About four years since it opened, the restaurant in Moscow's Pushkin Square generates sales volumes which are twelve times higher than that normal for outlets of its

---

[33]*Commersant,* September 22, 1993.

size. The restaurant caters for 40,000 guests each day. The Mac-Complex in Solntsevo processes 56,000 kg of beef per day, 72,000 kg potatoes, 90,000 litres of milk, 10,000 kg vegetables, 70,000 litres of sauce, bakes one million buns and cuts 130,000 slices of cheese. The JV has a staff of 1,900 of which only 10 are foreigners. 98 per cent of food products and other items needed in the restaurant are supplied locally.

The cornerstone of JV policy is to trade only in roubles. Although roubles revenue is substantial, it cannot cover the JV's hard currency expenses. However, the offices of the new Oganyovo Street building are rented to other foreign firms which brings in substantial hard currency revenues.

In 1993 the average Moscovite's monthly net income was only sufficient to buy 20-25 Big Macs. In spite of this figure, Moskva-McDonalds has calculated that their three restaurants will not be short of clients.[34]

In 1987 McDonalds established a JV in Hungary with a local partner which sold its share to McDonalds in 1992. In 1993 there were eleven McDonalds restaurants in Hungary. In Hungary too, 98 per cent of raw materials, packaging etc for McDonalds are supplied by local companies; but, unlike Moscow, there is no McDonalds own 'food town'. Suppliers must deliver everything according to detailed and strict prescriptions.

Out of eleven Hungarian McDonalds restaurants, five are operating on a franchise system. Franchise is a special kind of venture in which a contract for long-term co-operation is concluded between two legally independent parties. Within the provisions laid down in the contract, the franchisee is allowed to use the franchiser's trade name,

---

34 *Time Out in Moscow*, No 2, 1993.

equipment and exercise certain rights. The franchisee benefits from the McDonalds expertise and is helped by various departments such as Operations, Purchasing and Marketing. The entrepreneur must have the necessary starting capital and expertise. He will be the owner of a restaurant which has an international reputation; but he must undertake to comply with the strict and very high standard of requirements set by McDonalds.

McDonalds provides for the initiation of the franchise partners, the training of their staff, and advances some of the financial investment needed to start the new venture.

One of the main factors in McDonalds' success is the franchise system which is an efficient combination of the experience and research of a large company and the dynamism of a small enterprise. Today about 70 per cent of McDonalds restaurants in the world operate on a franchise system.

According to Mike Quinlan, Chairman of McDonalds, the first two restaurants in Poland have set records for customer traffic. However, he states that political uncertainties, limited consumer spending power, supply difficulties and the time needed to establish the McDonalds brand makes him cautious about the speed of future expansion in the developing world (TEs included). During this decade he is counting on Western Europe to act as the main engine of growth outside the US.[35]

Pepsi Cola, the soft drink which is popular in every country of the world - with the possible exception of North Korea - has now filtered down into the Moscow underground. The president of PepsiCo International's department for Eastern Europe and Central Asia, David Jones,

---

[35] *Financial Times*, October 18, 1993.

recently opened the first in a chain of kiosks called Metro Express, which will sell the products of PepsiCo and its subsidiary companies at stations of the Moscow Metro.

According to Mr Jones, the Metro Express network is unique in that it proposes to cover one of the largest underground transport systems in the world and offers a genuine 'American' service to over 8 million passengers who use the metro daily.

At the opening ceremony of the first Metro Express Kiosk at Park Kultury metro station, Mr Jones warmly embraced Yevgeny Dubchenko, the director-general of the Moscow metro, the organization which has undertaken to share with PepsiCo the risks involved in this huge venture. The Moscow metro was always considered a symbol of the indestructibility of socialist institutions and to this day is named in honour of Vladimir Lenin. It will now prove a channel not only for the endless stream of passengers but also for the fizzy brown liquid which is considered the symbol of the American way of life. Alongside Pepsi Cola, Metro Express kiosks will sell hot dogs, Mexican *burritos,* and Russian chicken-fried Kentucky style.

Pepsico's programme will provide jobs for some 6,000 Muscovites, and the profits from the Metro Express kiosks will be shared between PepsiCo and the Moscow metro at a ratio yet to be agreed. Judging by the number of people who queued to taste the products on sale at the kiosk on the first day, the venture will not be in any danger of making a loss.[36]

Not only fast food but also drinks seem to be a hot item in systemic transition in Eastern Europe. In the communist era, alcoholic beverages were produced on a mas-

---

[36] *Delovie Lyudi,* September, 1993.

sive scale. In the mid-1980s Mikhail Gorbachev decided that heavy drinking was one of the main reasons for low productivity in the Soviet economy and started severely limiting the supply of vodka. As a result, the demand for sugar sky-rocketed. No fundamental change in living habits was achieved.

Even during the time of central planning, some Eastern drinks maintained high quality. Russian Stolichnya Vodka was sold in the West. Czechoslovakian beer is sold under several famous and popular brands. Hungarian Tokaji wine was always available in the best restaurants.

It is clear that after the demise of communism Western drinks companies began to look for business opportunities in the East. They certainly assumed that drinking habits were not linked to the social system and that demand for drinks would be rather inelastic.

In this area various conflicts and disputes seem to have arisen. A new firm 'P A Smirnov and Descendants' has been set up in Moscow. This firm started to build a new distillery near the Russian city of Rostov. The owner, Boris Smirnov, says he is the only legitimate descendant of Peter Smirnov and claims the right to his recipes for the famous drink currently produced in the US. He said that producing Smirnov, or Smirnoff, vodka in the US was like producing Portuguese port wine in Malaysia, Scotch whisky in Africa or Jack Daniels in Europe.[37]

Scotch whisky seems already to have competitors elsewhere, according to *The Times*[38]. Within the past year, Johnnie Walker has been impersonated by look-alikes labelled Johnnie Hawker, Joe Worker and Johnnie Black. In

---

[37] *Financial and Business News from Moscow*, No 12, 1993.
[38] *The Times*, October 16, 1993.

Poland a group of people are awaiting trial accused of producing their own bottles, capsules and Johnnie Walker red and black labels. The 'whisky' sold in them was 3 per cent Scotch and the remainder 'local spirits of dubious origin', according to Guinness's United Distillers' spokesman.

Early in 1993, Hungarian State Property Agency (SPA) officials dropped a Western merchant bank as adviser on privatisation of K_bánya Sörgyár, Hungary's largest brewery. SPA said that the Western bank had invited bids for the brewery from three international companies which the government had specifically excluded from the sale tender. The SPA said that prospectuses for K_bánya went out to Interbrew, Heineken and Brau-Western brewers which have all already made investments and established strong market shares in Hungary - even though the SPA wanted to stop them making further acquisitions in the interests of competition. Mr Lajos Csepi, managing director of the SPA, said 'It is a very elementary mistake which cannot be explained'. This is the first time the SPA has publicly dismissed a consultant.

In November 1993, it was announced that South African Breweries (SAB), the country's largest consumer goods company, acquired an 80 per cent stake in K_bánya Sörgyár. SAB paid $50 million for its share and is committed to investing a further $40 million over a five-year period. K_bánya's capacity will be increased, particularly in the production of the brewery's 'Dreher' brand.[39]

In the autumn of 1993, BASS, the UK's leading brewer, agreed to acquire a 34 per cent stake in Prague Breweries, the second largest brewer in the Czech Republic, for £9

[39]*Financial Times*, November 18, 1993.

million. The deal is Bass's first overseas brewing venture since it sold its interest in Lamot, the Belgian brewer, 12 years ago.

Bass chairman and chief executive, Mr Ian Prosser, described the Prague deal as 'an important first step' in the group's moves towards international expansion and said it offered good prospects for further development in the Czech market and for increased exports.

The Prague group has a 10 per cent share of the Czech beer market, which is around one quarter of the size of the UK market. It will have net assets of £30 million after the deal is completed and plans to invest £50 million over the next five years in expansion and modernisation of its three breweries. Prague's sales in 1992 amounted to £36 million, which included a fair proportion from exports, mainly to Eastern and Central Europe.

Soon Bass will introduce Prague's leading premium lager, Staropramen, into the UK and a number of other international markets. The UK brewer will have four seats on the Prague board and a number of senior managers will be seconded to the group.[40]

Ottakringer Brauerei Harmer (Austria) has a fair amount of practice of licensing agreements: the company currently has agreements in place with brewers in Eastern Europe: in Poland, Slovenia and Hungary (with two partners), not to mention partners located further afield. In 1993 Ottakringer began producing its Goldfassl beer under licence at Saris, Slovakia's largest brewery, which has a capacity of 80,000 hl per year. .

To make sure of the continuous quality of output, specialists from the Austrian company will both supervise the

[40] *Financial Times*, November 2, 1993.

licensing operation in its start-up phase and also remain as an integral part of the local brewer's management and production process. Beside providing Saris with its brewery technology and know-how, Ottakringer will give the company assistance in the areas of marketing and sales and offer financing.

Although many such licensing agreements are concluded because of low East European labour costs. Ottakringer states that the argument for going into local production is based on the nature of its product, which is expensive to transport.

It was estimated that by the end of 1993, the Saris brewery would have sold some 30,000 hl, increasing its sales volume to 100,000 hl this year and 200,000 hl within three years. Saris will also export Goldfassl beer produced at the Slovak brewery to customers in the Czech Republic, Poland and Ukraine through its existing distribution channels.[41]

Sweden's largest beer and soft-drink manufacturer, Pripps Beverages, was the third Western company to bid for a chunk of privatized property in St Petersburg.

In 1993 the Baltic Beverages Holdings investment company, in which Pripps has a share, bought the controlling interest in the Baltika brewery. Baltika was built in 1990 and uses Czech equipment to produce four different beers. Its projected capacity is 10 million decaliters a year.

Pripps followed both Finland's Sinebryhoff, which bought the controlling interest in the Vena brewery, and Holsten, which has its eyes on the Stepan Razin factory. The Swedish company are keen to establish themselves in

---

[41] *Business Eastern Europe,* September 27, 1993.

northern Russia. Before the end of 1993, Pripps beer was being sold in fifty outlets in St Petersburg.[42]

Not only in drinks production, but also in public houses there is keen Western interest in emerging TE-markets:

The John Bull Pub Kft. is a Hungarian joint venture which was established in 1990 with initial capital of HUF 30 billion. It is held 50 per cent by the British Allied Retailing, a member company of Allied Lyons Holding. The other 50 per cent is held by the Hungarian Foreign Trade Bank and the Hungarian Consultrade. Their eighth pub in Hungary was opened in Budapest in July 1993 and there are plans to establish a franchise chain of forty pubs in Hungary. Four hundred barrels of beer a week are imported from Scotland. A total of GBP 800,000 had already been invested in the chain.[43]

A myriad of interesting deals were concluded in the communist period between Eastern and Western companies in the sphere of labour intensive consumer goods production; in textiles, clothing and footwear. Levi Strauss started producing in Hungary in the mid-1970s and later established a JV with a local partner. The German company 'Triumph' (ladies underwear) also operated in Hungary. Salamander, the German footwear manufacturer established a JV in Leningrad during the communist period.[44]

Many of these deals were based on the buy-back system. In other words, a proportion of the goods manufac-

---

[42]*Commersant*, August 4 1993.

[43]*Hungarian Economic Review*, October 1993.

[44]For details, see Tiusanen: *Western Direct Investments in European CMEA Countires in the 1970s and 1980s* , Helsinki, 1990.

tured in the East were exported to the West. This popular method had obvious advantages for the Eastern partner which was able to pay the Western firm with goods and thus save hard currency. The Western partner normally profited from the cheap labour costs in the East. When part of the produce remained on the local market, the Western company was able to get a foothold in the East where purchasing power was, and still is, relatively low. Producing the goods locally made them more affordable for the local population in comparison with direct imports from the West.

These economic background factors are still valid. Now, after the systemic change in the Eastern economies, it can be assumed that Western companies are now more inclined to make an FDI than before.

Elit's Székesfehérvár plant was about to close down when its performance attracted two potential foreign partners: a British firm that bought the entire Elit, and an Italian-Hungarian joint venture.The Székesfehérvár plant of Elit is now a British-Hungarian joint-stock company and has been rented by the Italian-Hungarian Dunafashion Kereskedelmi és Szolgáltató Kft since June 1, 1993.

The company, supplies the Italian market and has long-term plans in Székesfehérvár: they installed some twenty machines and irons totalling HUF 5 million in the first six months, and the workers - who were given a 50 per cent pay rise - have been officially employed by Dunafashion since June 1993. The factory produced 22,000 jackets and 8000 pairs of trousers in its first six months and these were sold on the Hungarian, Italian and US markets.[45]

---

[45] *Hungarian Economic Review*, October 1993.

In the summer of 1993, Russia's Vostok watchmaker was granted a three-year contract which gave it exclusive rights to market its famous Red Army watches to Switzerland's BN-Trading. Vostok, which is based in the city of Chistopol, will supply 500,000 watches a year to the Swiss trading firm. Vostok director, Vladislav Tsivilin, hoped that co-operation with BN-Trading would help combat the competition from makers of counterfeit Red Army watches.

Tsivilin complained that the demand for Russian military watches had led to the production of clones by many unscrupulous small watchmaking companies. Vostok could do little to prevent this and it seems that inferior counterfeits were being hawked to buyers in Europe, America and Japan.

BN-Trading agreed to market 'Commander', 'General', 'Admiral' and 'KGB' models made by Vostok under its trademark and will also advertise Vostok's watches outside of Russia.

The 'Commander' watches made by Vostok became fashionable in 1989 and have been in constant demand ever since, with sales reaching up to 200,000 a year in the United States, Japan and Western Europe. Hard currency revenues earned from such sales enabled Vostok to boost production of these watches to three million per year.[46]

Originally a Czech company, BATA, one of the worlds leading shoe manufacturers - selling 300m pairs of shoes per year, operating in 65 countries and employing 70,000 people - has returned to invest in its native country.

At the end of 1991 the company took over 29 state owned shops and a factory at a cost of $10m. Since then

---

[46]*Commersant*, July 7 1993.

the number of outlets has increased to 43. At present the company has a 1 per cent share of the Czech market and is facing considerable competition from Italian and Austrian companies.

The main manufacturing plant at Dolni Nemci has been extensively modernised and the workers retrained. BATA looks set to increase its investment by purchasing the option on the remaining plants of Svit - the largest footwear company in the Czech republic.

Despite these advances there have been considerable problems in securing suppliers to conform to BATAs high standard. Thus soles are imported from Italy. However, with modernisation and retraining it is likely that more domestic suppliers will be used.

BATA has the advantage of being well known in the Czech market as a Czech company. Its high profile chairman Tomas Bata - a Czech exile is as well known in the country as leading political figures. Though some thorny questions of recompense for BATA properties expropriated by the communists remain there can be little doubt that the company will continue to made inroads into the Czech and central and east European markets.[47]

---

[47] *Business Central Europe,* October 1993.

CHAPTER FOUR

4. The Future of FDIs in TEs

As highlighted in the previous chapter, the impact of FDIs on TEs has not been substantial during the first years of transition. Obviously from the point of view of TE-economic policy makers, the results have been disappointing. At the same time, there have been circles in TEs worried about being 'taken over' by foreign investors resulting in the Central and East European countries becoming, effectively, the economic statellites of Western powers.

Some tendencies in TE development in the mid-1990s were scarcely predictable five years ago. It was generally assumed that the so-called shock-therapy with its quick-fix alternatives was the best medicine for the ailing economies in the East. This therapy was supposed to be painful in terms of decreasing economic activity but it was said to be the short-term price worth paying for a bright capitalist future. The first years of transition have shown that the pain was more severe than was generally expected, and that there are, therefore, political tendencies visible in TEs which have puzzled the Western world: neo-communist and neo-fascist (especially Vladimir

Zhirinovsky's success in the Russian elections in 1993) movements have demonstrated their strengths. The main reason for this tendency is obviously the fact that capitalism in its early stage has meant more pain than gain for the majority of the populations in TEs.

In the meantime, some scholars in the West have started wondering whether the Western model of liberal capitalism can be applied at all in TEs. Is the cultural shock of transition manageable or not? If it cannot be digested by the TEs, what is the alternative?

This question is of utmost importance from the point of view of Western investors who plan to commit their assets on a long-term basis in TEs. It is discussed below in the section on 'investment climate' in TEs. and some aspects of the neo-communist and neo-fascist tendencies in TEs will be addressed in the same section.

In respect of FDIs, one of the biggest problems in the early 1990s has been the recession affecting OECD countries. With economic slowdown at home, many Western firms have not been well placed to invest abroad. However, the recession of the early 1990s in the West was very mild indeed when compared to the slump experienced by TEs in the same period. This serious economic setback in TEs, which certainly was one of the reasons for the reluctance of foreign investors to enter the TE-market, is discussed in section 4.2. In the same context, economic growth prospects in TEs are discussed in order to see whether more dynamism can be expected in TEs and, thus, more opportunities for FDIs.

There is a myriad of reasons why FDIs take place on a vast scale in the modern global economy. No attempt to explain all of them is undertaken here. It is an undisputed fact that FDIs can be seen as a reaction to trade policy. American firms in the 1960s and Japanese companies in the 1980s supposedly invested in Europe to counter the uncertainty over EC trade policy. The correspondence in time between shifts in EC policies and inward investment into the EC has lent support to this hypothesis. At the same time, the removal of internal barriers as part of the single market initiative is widely regarded as a driving force behind FDIs in Europe in the late 1980s; as firms restructured to take advantage of greater cost savings through economies of scale. The failure to restructure earlier is attributed to the lack of a credible commitment to the Single Market.[48]

Trade policy issues are of vital importance for TEs which are trying to attract FDIs on an increasing scale. Therefore, section 4.3 deals with the topic of trade policy and describes TEs' links with the EU (formerly the EC) at present and speculates on the possibilities of pan-European integration.

There are some clear attractions for foreign investors in TEs. One of these is the relatively cheap labour costs and abundant natural resources which are, however unevenly distributed, to be found TEs. Cheap labour and low purchasing power are two sides of the same coin. FDIs are obviously less and less determined by cheap labour and availability of local raw materials and more and more attracted by high purchasing power in FDIs host countries.

---

[48]S Thomsen and S Woolcock: *Direct Investment and European Integration: Competition Among Firms and Governments*, London, 1993 p.39.)

4.1 The 'investment climate' in TEs

There is a great variety of historical and cultural backgrounds to be found in the different TEs under review (former European CMEA-countries, including former Soviet republics). No attempt is made here to go into the details of this, despite the fact that it is a fascinating area of interest. Only some minor points, which are linked to the 'economic culture' of communist and post communist societies, are taken up, and these in a very general way.

The central planning system, which prevailed in the former Soviet Union for over 70 years and in other former CMEA countries for more than 40 years, has left some managerial attitudes which are similar in all TEs. These behavioural models can be summed up as follows:

(i) a low level both of skill-specific training for managerial and business activity and of basic economic knowledge (the majority of State enterprise general managers and general managers' deputies have received an engineer's education);

(ii) a lack of competence in special economic problems, resulting in their wish to pass the functions of performing technical and economic calculations, preparing contracts, regulating internal staff relations to economists and legal advisers of the lowest level. As a consequence preparing decisions and making decisions are separated;

(iii) a defensive attitude towards innovations in the economic sphere, because they are aware of their own incompetence.

Under these conditions the phenomenon of 'private property in the work place' and the aspiration to maximize personal income leads to management decisions that are irrational from the standpoint of the enterprises' interests: for example, intensive international negotiations (especially on the part of the 'second echelon' managers) are accompanied by frequent business trips abroad, payment of per diem expenses and receipt of gifts (sometimes equivalent to several months' salary).

The traditional type of state enterprise managers' economic behaviour corresponds to the conditions of the command economy based on shortage and cannot be changed overnight. For example, it might be expressed in the hoarding of natural resources (stocks of raw materials and equipment exceeding any standard, excessive facilities, excessive labour force). As a result, the behaviour of State enterprise leaders in a market economy is usually irrational. Thus, if traditional outlets (provided by a branch ministry) are no longer available a typical decision may be to reduce output, rather than to seek new outlets.[49]

Kuzminov makes some important points in an article, which was written in the early stage of the transition, concerning negative aspects of the new system. The following remarks have a universal validity in TEs:

> Mass consciousness is beginning to react negatively to the commercial structures and business initiative existing in the USSR: (a) most citizens as consumers derive no benefit from the activity of new structures because those on relatively low incomes and without

---

[49] J Kuzminov: 'Transition to a Market Economy and the Problems of Changing the Economic Culture', in *European Economy: Reform Issues in the former Soviet Union* ,Commission of European Communities No 49/1993. Brussels, 1993)

> access to hard currency still face shortages; (b) against the background of shortages of basic consumer goods and growing absolute impoverishment, conspicuous consumption by those employed in the free sectors causes great irritation; economic success appears to be random: access to the highly profitable sector does not depend on achieving a high professional level, nor on working diligently, and high profits are also haphazard. There is no positive image of a businessman as a hard worker, but there is an image of a businessman (and his dependants) as 'playboys'.
>
> We may face the danger of a dual social-economic structure of society with an isolated sphere of leisure, shops, way of life and, moreover, with entry apparently barred to the rest of society. It is worth remembering that a similar situation occurred in the 1920s during the 'new economic policy' period, and in the long run it brought about social tension which became one of the leading forces causing the closing down of private and commercial structures and the transition to a command economy.

Development of natural property differences into those of class and caste may obliterate the positive image of a market economy that resulted from the destruction of state socialism. The risk will be intensified if conditions of impoverishment cause access to education to become the monopoly of the rich and powerful.[50]

This citation contains several reasons why there is some nostalgia for the old system which is also visible in the political scene: reformers are not being strongly endorsed by the electorate.

Some Western observers are extremely pessimistic concerning the systemic change in TEs. John Gray of Oxford rejects as unfeasible and undesirable the notion that

---

[50] *Ibid.*

Western exemplars of market institutions can be transplanted to the historical circumstance of post-communist countries.[51] For Gray, the idea that there is a special or universal connection between flourishing market institutions and an individualistic cultural tradition is an historical myth, an element in recent neo-conservative folklore, especially in the United States, rather than the result of any disciplined historical or sociological investigation[52].

Gray argues that the development paths of market institutions in other parts of the world, and in other historical milieux, cannot be replicated or tracked anywhere in the post-communist world, because the inheritance of central planning does not vanish with the regimes which sponsored it. It lingers on pervasively, not only as habits of thought and expectation in the population, and as coalitions of groups with diverse and often conflicting interests in the market reform process, but also as physical plant, as logistical and distribution systems, as energy supply arrangements and - last but not least - as a terrible inheritance of pollution and environmental degradation. This inherited deformation of the institutional and natural environments is, according to Gray, a common feature of every TE, whatever their many differences may be[53].

Gray concludes in his pamphlet that the Soviet collapse, far from enhancing the stability of Western institutions, has destabilised them by knocking away the strategic props on which they stood. The prospects of the orderly integration of TEs into the economic and security ar-

---

[51] J Gray: *Post-communist Societies in Transiton: A Social Market Perspective*. London, 1994.
[52] *Ibid.*, p.31.
[53] *Ibid.*, p.29.

rangements of the Western world is a mirage, not only because of the unprecedentedly formidable difficulties each of them confronts in its domestic development, but because the major Western transnational institutions and organisations are themselves in a flux, and some may even cease to operate. If there is a global trend that is presently afoot, it may well be one in which economic initiative is shifting from the Western nations, from whose historical experience standard economic theory takes its bearings, to the non-Occidental cultures of East Asia. In this larger historical context, the Soviet collapse will be seen not as another surge in an irresistible movement of Westernization but as the beginning of the world-historical reversal of that movement. In that event, Western theoretical models and Western market institutions themselves will confront many serious problems of adjustment.[54]

Gray does not develop the various scenarios for post-communist development paths, though he warns against the illusions Western politicians and businessmen seem to have concerning the quick and smooth transition in TEs. It is not surprising that TEs have been in an institutional halfway house between two economic systems in the early stage of the transition. This situation has been well described by A Kuznetsov who observes the 'investment climate in post-communist Russia.[55]

> The positive changes have most of all affected what can conditionally be called the higher levels of policy. Lower levels, i.e., the way the government ideology is applied, have remained less

---

[54]ibid, p.41.

[55]A Kuznetsov: *Foreign Investment in Contemporary Russia*. London, 1994, 106-107).

affected. In the actions of the present government of Russia ostentatious liberalism has coexisted in a picturesque manner with unceremonious administration, leaving foreign experts wondering which of the two represented the authentic concept of government policy concept. In practical terms this inconsistency in regulation passes much of the actual decision-making power on to ministries and their substitutes, and other lower levels of economic authority. They played an important role in the previous system, but lately have been losing importance, and their prospects and future role are unclear. As a result they still retain some levers of control, although their formal responsibility for the performance of the economy has almost vanished. This transitional situation has created a climate of low executive morality and illegal actions. Corruption and the shadow economy have developed to such an extent that they have ceased to be simply events in a criminal chronicle. They have instead become so much a fact of investment climate and policy risk that only a rare domestic or international press publication on foreign investment in the CIS does not comment on this subject. Foreign investors complain that their projects falter because of excessive red-tape and unmotivated last-moment changes in contract conditions with Russian officials seeming to be more interested in new trips abroad than in the results of the talks...

Liberal economic policy can bring results when it relies on an extensive market mechanism and the authority of the law. Both are missing in modern Russia. It would not be right to claim that the Yeltsin/Gaidar government did not realise this. On the contrary, the importance of functioning market relations as a foundation for efficient state and civil society was repeatedly stressed by government spokesmen as a motivation for drastic reforms. Still a conflict between liberalism and administrating represented one of the main problems of the regime. It was not only the question of imposing the freedom of enterprise by way of command. It is also characteristic that the accentuated liberalism of many important

> government decisions appeared good on paper, but in reality only gave more space for administrative arbitrariness.[56]

One of the main difficulties foreign business people are facing in TEs is pointed out by Kuznetsov: theory and practice do not necessarily overlap in TEs' institutional framework. 'Learning by doing' is one of the applicable methods available for foreign investors: this comment is often made by Westerners who run enterprises in TEs.

Some institutional aspects of the 'business climate' in TEs have been covered in this section in a very general way. It is worth noting that in the mid-90s TEs can no longer be treated as a bundle of hopeless economies. The economic picture is increasingly diversified in the TE region. This is very visible in the light of economic performance, which is highlighted in the next section, which shows that relative economic stability combined with economic growth is not necessarily a dream only in TEs.

4.2. Economic Growth in TEs

The euphoria which greeted the collapse of the communist regimes and central planning in TEs quickly gave way to a more sober assessment of the problems involved in fostering the systemic change. With continuing large falls in output and private consumption, rising unemployment and high rates of inflation, there has been an increase in social discontent and disillusionment.

In the three-year period 1990-92, GDP declined by some 27 per cent in the TE region and industrial production even more - by some 40 per cent. Real incomes radi-

---

[56] *Ibid.*

cally decreased, especially for wage-earners, and unemployment - almost unknown in the region before the 1990s - increased. It is appropriate to speak about post-communist depression or slump, instead of 'recession'. Obviously, the TE slump during 1990-92, so far as its depth and protraction in most TEs is concerned, is unmatched even by the Great Depression of 1929-1933 in the West.

It should be pointed out that falls in output in TEs exaggerate the decline in economic welfare in so far as part of the lost production consists of goods for which there was no demand. It can be assumed that the expansion of private sector output has been imperfectly portrayed in the official statistics. However, it is impossible to quantify these qualifications.

During these difficult first years of transition, there has been no excessive inflationary wave in Czechoslovakia and Hungary. In the latter this is attributed to the fact that Hungarian economic reforms began well before the systemic change took place. In Czechoslovakia, where strict central planning ruled until 1989, the market obviously was in better equilibrium than in the other CMEA countries. Both Hungary and Czechoslovakia have suffered considerable setbacks in production in 1990-92. No great differences in output declines are visible between these two countries.

The sharp economic decline in 1990-92 and the resultant obvious deterioration of living standards is to a large part a consequence of austerity policy. Governments in TEs have been facing serious problems in their economic policy-making. Increasing unemployment has caused supplementary social costs which must be covered from the budget in which revenues have decreased due to the slump and far-reaching tax evasion. At the same time, there is an urgent need to control the budget deficit: the IMF demands that TEs keep their budget deficits below 5 per cent of GNP. As IMF loans are conditional - depending on the application of IMF advice - there has been very little scope for expansionary economic policy. Moreover any relaxation in economic policy obviously enhances the possibility of continuously strong inflation.

On the other hand, the lasting and severe decline in output may endanger the systemic change, defined as the development of institutions of the market and market-type relations. There is an obvious danger that old structures of the economy come to an end without new structures coming in to replace them. In a weak TE, a continuous sharp decline in domestic demand may create intractable adjustment difficulties, not only for the state-owned sector with its traditional rigidity, but also for the newly developing private sector. This is because there is not necessarily enough capital on acceptable terms to finance business start-up or enough customers capable of paying reasonable prices to ensure that the new outlets become profitable. There is thus the possibility that the economy will enter a vicious circle of decline.

Therefore, TE economic development is like dancing on a tightrope: macro-economic stabilization must be achieved in order to create preconditions for healthy growth, while long-lasting austerity may postpone the start of a badly needed recovery and prosperity. The first three years of post-communism have shown that it is possible to find a reasonable economic policy mix under difficult TE circumstances, even where no universally applicable ideal transition model has come into being. The second three-year period of post-communist development is of vital importance for the future of the TE region.

The early experience of the former centrally planned economies has clearly demonstrated that a severe slump in economic activity cannot be avoided. The early shock of the systemic change has also resulted in a strong inflationary wave in all TEs which, in itself, is a natural result of moving from repressed to open inflation. At the same time, choice, accessibility and quality of goods and services have begun to improve. This means that forced substitution in consumption and production (replacement of shortage goods by those available) involving long queues, forced savings, inventories of useless goods etc., are beginning to disappear.

After the first shock of structural reform it is crucially important to reach a consolidation phase in which relative macro-economic stabilization is established. However, this phase seems to be difficult to reach and sustain in the presence of strong temptations to run the large fiscal deficits that have accompanied the considerable losses of output and tax revenue since the start of the reform process. The transformation process is in many cases being seriously hampered by the widespread subsidisation of inefficient enterprises and the resulting misallocation of resources.

Economic results of 1993 show a clearly diversified picture of economic development in the TE region. The Czech Republic, Hungary and Poland have made the greatest progress in macroeconomic stabilization and structural reform. In these countries there are clear signs that output is recovering and that inflationary pressure is abating. As the reforms already in place begin to take hold, and assuming that further reforms are carried out as planned, and that inflation is contained, real output growth is expected to rise during the rest of the decade.

TEs economic development in 1993-94 (1994 forecast)

	GDP real change %		Inflation %		Unemployment %	
	1993	1994	1993	1994	1993	1994
Czech Republic	-1.0	2	20.8	11	3.5	7
Hungary	-2.0	1	22.5	23	12.1	13
Poland	4.0	4	35.3	30	15.7	17
Slovak Republic	-4.1	-2	23.2	20	14.4	18
Bulgaria	-4.8	-2	72.9	55	16.4	18
Romania	-1.0	-1	256.1	200	10.2	12
Russia	-12.0	-7	930	500	1.2	2
Ukraine	-15.0	-12	3700	1000	0.4	3

Source: WIIW

Poland is the first country in the TE region to have achieved clear economic growth which accelerated from 1 per cent in 1992 (GDP) to some 4 per cent in 1993; the highest GDP growth in Europe in that year. Poland managed to keep its budget deficit within the 5 per cent (of GDP) limit agreed with the IMF, although tax evasion was still a major problem.

It can be stated, therefore, that in the case of Poland the application of shock therapy has started to pay off. However, the social costs of the restructuring have been considerable. The rate of unemployment rose from 13.5 per cent in 1992 to 15.7 per cent in 1993. At the same time, real wages went down by some 2 per cent. The total number of unemployed reached 2.8 million.

There are signs in Poland of a decline in the rate of unemployment as private firms absorb growing numbers of workers laid off in the state sector. The annual inflation rate, which was about 46 per cent in 1992, has shown a decreasing tendency and was about 30 per cent in 1993 - still a relatively high figure by international comparison. The nominal depreciation of the Z_oty (Polish currency) was a little less than the inflation rate (28 per cent), and thus the real exchange rate experienced a slight appreciation.

The relatively strong economic upturn in Poland was therefore combined with a tendency towards equilibrium in the internal economy. Increasing demand caused a clear increase in imports, while exports showed only very moderate growth.

Foreign direct investments did not increase greatly during 1993, but a new phenomenon on the Polish market appeared, namely portfolio investors who helped to finance the upturn and to prevent the depletion of currency reserves.

Obviously, there is a real danger that the sustainability of the Polish boom depends now on the ability to maintain the relative balance of the external economy. A balance of payments constraint is looming as the post-communist boom in Poland gains momentum.

In any event, Poland can be described as a positive case of post-communist transition which enters first an unavoidable transitional slump with strong inflation, but which has been able to reach a consolidation phase with an already fairly well balanced economy in a relatively short period. It is widely expected that the Polish economy is now entering a recovery phase with growth rates of 4-5 per cent each year.

The Czech Republic, established in 1993 when the former Czechoslovakia was dismantled, gave a rather successful economic performance during its first year of existence. Although there was still no clear upturn in economic activity in 1993, the unemployment rate was amazingly low at only 3.5 per cent. This is an exceptional result in a country where privatization has advanced very quickly.

There have been several factors affecting the positive development of the labour market. There has been a government-led prevention of bankruptcy; labour costs are very low and their rapid increase was stalled by reintroducing strict wage controls for all companies with more than twenty-five employees; Czech exports experienced a strong boom; and tourist revenues increased markedly.

The consolidation of the Czech economy is not, however, going forward without hindrance. There is, as in all TEs - the phenomenon of inter-enterprise debt which must be abolished. Additional capital must be freed up in the economy to solve the bad debt crisis or the liquidation of insolvent firms must start in earnest. The present consolidation phase has only postponed this fundamental question of 'structural cleansing' in order to avoid unemployment increasing.

Czechoslovakia did not experience any extreme inflationary period during the first years of transition. In the Czech Republic there was certainly no danger of hyperinflation during 1993, but consumer prices increased by some

20 per cent which is a high figure by international comparison. The exchange rate remained virtually unchanged in 1993, which means that the Czech fixed exchange rate regime has allowed the Koruna (the Czech monetary unity) to appreciate clearly in real terms.

It is obvious that the Czech approach of relative gradualism has brought about relatively impressive results, and that the economy is poised to enter a recovery phase in the mid-1990s. However, a coherent industrial policy is now needed in order to find an optimum solution to poorly-performing companies. Sustainable economic growth presupposes the freeing up of resources for viable and dynamic enterprises. Under the present circumstances, scarce capital is not optimally allocated.

At the beginning of the post-communist era, it was generally anticipated that Hungary, because of the economic reforms enacted during the communist period, would have a relatively easy task in transforming its economy. Therefore, it is somewhat surprising that Hungary had a hard struggle to consolidate its economy and begin a phase of recovery which was still not clearly under way in 1993.

There were some specific reasons why the recovery of the Hungarian economy was hindered. Agriculture performed badly, mainly due to adverse weather conditions. Agricultural and food exports decreased by one third in 1993. The unofficial or 'black' economy is burgeoning and makes up an estimated one quarter of the overall economic activity. Thus, official figures give a relatively biased picture of the economic scene.

Budgetary problems are compounded by the high level of tax evasion. There is a real danger that the budget deficit cannot be squeezed under the 5 per cent limit (of the GDP) set by the IMF.

The unemployment rate remained on the same 12 per cent level in 1993 as it had one year earlier. No real improvement in inflation rates were achieved: consumer prices increased some 23 - 24 per cent in both 1992 and 1993. Obviously, relatively high budget deficits are fuelling the inflationary trend.

In 1993, Hungary faced a clear balance of trade problem after the relative equilibrium of 1992. The trade deficit was an estimated $2.5 billion. At the same time, Hungary remained the largest recipient of foreign direct investments in Eastern Europe; although there was no increase in FDI inflow in comparison with 1992.

Labour costs (calculated in hard currency) are much higher than in the neighbouring TEs. Therefore, it is not self-evident that Hungary can attract more FDIs than other TEs during the coming years. It is likely that the Hungarian Forint must be devalued at a faster rate than in the 1991-1993 period. Three separate devaluations took place in 1994.

Romania's and Bulgaria's reform efforts have been halfheartedly implemented. Both countries still struggle with the macroeconomic stabilization. In 1993 inflation in Romania was some 240 per cent while the Bulgarian figure was 70 per cent. Both countries are also suffering from high unemployment.

Slovakia, which faced more problems than the Czech Republic after the break-up of the federation, has been reluctant to embrace reform. Slovakia's economy is, therefore, facing a number of uncertainties.

There are forecasts which predict that a post-communist growth period in TEs outside the former Soviet Union (FSU) will begin in 1994 and last through the remaining years of the 1990s. There are, however, many uncertainties in TEs which can easily affect the predicted trend.

It can be roughly estimated that the economic activity in TEs (without FSU) has dropped about one quarter during the immediate post-communist slump. In the table below calculations for three recovery scenarios for the previous 'small' CMEA countries are shown.

Calculated recovery of TEs (without FSU)
GDP 1989 = 100, 1993 = 75

Year	Annual Growth Rate		
	3%	5%	8%
1993	75	75	75
1994	77.3	78.8	81.0
1995	79.6	82.7	87.5
1996	82.0	86.8	94.5
1997	84.5	91.1	102.1
1998	87.0	95.7	110.3
1999	89.6	100.5	119.1
2000	92.3	105.5	128.6
2001	95.1	110.8	138.9
2002	98.0	116.3	150.0
2003	100.9	122.1	162.0

If a new sustainable growth period starts in 1994 and if average annual growth rate in the region under review will be 3 per cent, then the level of economic activity reached in 1989 - the last 'communist year - will be re-established first in the year 2003!

The column in middle of the table shows the most realistic scenario in calculating on an annual average growth rate of 5 per cent. In this case it will take until the end of the 1990s to catch up with the level of the end of the 1980s. Only in the next century will economic activity achieve the levels reached during the communist era. However, the type of economy which is at present emerging in the post-communist era will be qualitatively different from the inefficient, wasteful system characteristic of economic development under communism (see below).

In the short term, a vigorous annual growth rate of 8 per cent is needed to eliminate the negative influence of the slump of the early 1990s. In this scenario the level of 1989 would be surpassed in 1997. The scenario is obviously over optimistic: 8 per cent economic growth is not forecast for the smaller former Comecon countries in the 1990s.

In this context it is necessary to make some comments on the old system where there was a chronic tendency towards imbalance, unwillingness of enterprises to innovate, pervasive inefficiencies and system wide indifference to customers. Because of these deficiencies of the system, its ultimate collapse was unavoidable.

In central planning, relative prices were fixed at inappropriate levels and did not represent relative costs; which led to a sub-optimal allocation of given resources. Therefore, the systemic change in TEs is supposed to introduce flexible prices determined by relative scarcity and to improve the allocation of endowments and thereby, the prosperity level of the society. There are striking examples of mis-allocation. For example, because the level of domestic energy price was far below that of world market prices, the centrally planned economies have wasted an enormous amount of energy. Since, simultaneously, different administrative exchange rates were used, it became possible for the prices of final products sold on the world market to be lower than the cost of intermediate products bought on the same world market needed to produce these final products. According to a recent estimate, 20-25 per cent of the manufacturing in Poland, former Czechoslovakia and Hungary consisted of such value subtractions.[57] It can be assumed that the situation in other TEs was similar or even worse.

Therefore, economic activity figures for the late 1980s only incompletely reflected the actual prosperity levels in TEs. This fact must be taken into consideration when comparisons are done with figures from the 1980s and 1990s: quantitative figures give too positive a picture of the communist era.

However, the calculated recovery scenarios above show how severe the slump in the TEs (without the FSU) during the early 1990s has been and how time-consuming it is to re-establish the previous level of economic activity. Even if an annual average growth of 5 per cent in the region as a whole were to be achieved, there is not yet enough leeway for an increase in overall living-standards. Improvements must come from the qualitative side of restructuring: production, based on excessive waste of resources and which is largely unrelated to use-values, must

---

57 P Hare and G Hughes: *Competitiveness and Industrial Restructuring in Czechoslovakia, Hungary and Poland*. Centre for Economic Policy Research, London 1991).

be replaced by goods and services which have a market price and are of acceptable quality for the client.

In the FSU, where the transition process started with a time lag in comparison to other former CMEA countries, the consolidation phase has proved extremely difficult to achieve. There are a few exceptions, particularly Estonia. In 1993 the two major economies of the region, Russia and the Ukraine, produced very poor results. In both countries attempts to reach macro-economic stabilization during the first two years have failed. The Ukraine has definitely reached a phase which can be characterized by the word 'hyperslumpflation' - a deep slump combined with an uncontrollable inflation.

In Russia recession slowed down somewhat from a drop in the GDP to some 20 per cent in 1992 to some 12 per cent in 1993. Yet recession continued in every sphere of the economy. Economic activity was some 42 per cent below the 1990 level. This catastrophic fall in output has not yet produced any mass unemployment because market forces do not yet operate properly in the sphere of labour. The workforce has so far been extremely immobile, while output per worker (productivity) has dropped dramatically.

In 1993 economic activity in the FSU (excluding the Baltic States) was about 55 per cent of the level in 1990. If we assume that a consolidation is taking place in 1994-95, with output still falling in 1994, it is possible to produce calculated growth scenarios for the second half of the 1990s.

Calculated recovery of FSU
(excluding the Baltic States)
GDP 1990 = 100
1994 = 50

Year	3%	5%	8%	10%	15%
1995	51.5	52.5	54.0	55.0	57.5
1996	53.0	55.1	58.3	60.5	66.1
1997	54.6	57.9	63.0	66.6	76.0
1998	56.2	60.8	68.0	73.3	87.4
1999	57.9	63.8	73.4	80.6	100.5
2000	59.6	67.0	79.3	88.7	115.6
2001	61.4	70.4	85.6	97.6	132.9
2002	63.2	73.9	92.4	107.4	152.8
2003	65.1	77.6	99.8	118.1	175.7
2004	67.1	81.5	107.8	129.9	202.1
2005	69.1	85.6	116.4	142.9	232.4

It is likely that the economic activity in the FSU in 1994 will be only about half of the 1990 level. If a moderate growth of 3 per cent per annum begins in 1995, the pre-crisis level of 1990 will first be achieved in the year 2019! An annual growth of 5 per cent will bring about the same result in 2009, while 8 per cent yearly growth would be needed to meet the 1990 level by 2003. Not even a 10 per cent growth rate would be sufficient to re-establish the pre-crisis economic activity in this century. A 15 per cent growth rate would be only just sufficient.

It is self-evident that in the FSU case also, the earlier remarks on misallocation of resources must be taken into consideration: there was a continuous 'soft budget constraint' in respect of investment behaviour which caused consistent over-investment combined with low productivity. There are many studies which estimate that total factor productivity decreased significantly during the last two decades of Soviet power. The revival of investment, combined with adequate efficiency criteria, are crucial to economic growth in the FSU. However, if the famous 'soft budget constraint' in the enterprise sector is revived with lax financial and monetary policies, it is possible that a new period of growth without a clear link to improving living-standards will come about.

The table of calculated growth scenarios for FSU illustrates the severity of the slump in the first half of the 1990s in that region. Given an average 5 per cent annual growth rate, it would take around one and a half decades to re-establish the level of economic activity of 1990; it is highly unlikely that a faster growth rate of 8, 10 or 15 per cent per annum can be regarded as realistic.

It is not commonly realized in the West just how deep the slump in TEs, especially in FSU, has been and how high the 'social costs' of transition were. These high social costs reflect results in the political sphere; reformist governments, even where they have been as successful as in Poland, are not necessarily popular. Under the hard conditions of post-communism there is an extremely fertile political market for populism, the colour of which cannot be easily predicted. It is also understandable that an uneven distribution of the fruits of economic reforms intensifies social tension and thus gives nourishment to populism.

Very little attention has been paid in the West to the fact that the disintegration of the Soviet economy has been basically an insurmountable problem for the whole of the

FSU. Russia is in possession of most of the strategically important raw materials and energy inherited from the Soviet era. During the first two years of the post-Soviet period, the republics have had only limited success in fighting for economic independence. The creation of a new economic order within the framework of the FSU is fraught with friction and tension.

It is impossible to predict the consequences of the dominant Russian position in the economic development of the FSU. In 1992-93 Russia has granted credits to the other republics by supplying goods for which no payment has been received. There is little willingness on the part of Russia to continue bearing that burden in future.

It is of utmost importance to realise that a return to the old system is only possible in Russia and those TEs which are willing to establish close links with Russia. Only Russia has the resource base for the wasteful system of central planning, in which large numbers of enterprises subtract value rather than add value. If resources are imported on a large scale - as during the 'good old Comecon days' in the 'small' CMEA countries - and then value is subtracted from imported materials and energy, the result will be an unmanageable balance of payments crisis. There is no economic unit in the world which would be willing to bear the costs of that kind of an external disequilibrium. Out of political considerations, the Soviet Union shouldered the burden and subsidised its allies during the oil crises. But Russia has shown an unwillingness to do that continuously vis-a-vis the other Soviet republics.

The most publicised economic detail concerning TEs in 1993 was the 4 per cent economic growth figure achieved in Poland, which was said by the Western media to be the highest in the whole of Europe. This figure is undoubtedly good news and shows that radical shock therapy really can pay off and create preconditions for healthy economic development. However, this Polish performance must be seen in its proper long-term context.

In the long-term it is necessary to establish a market-oriented price system with proper efficiency criteria and to achieve relative macro-economic stability as a basis for a sustainable economic growth. After that a growth period of several decades is needed, with annual growth rates of some 4 - 6 per cent a year, in order to reach the living-standards of the Western Europe of the late 1980s which was one of the original aims of anti-communist revolutions in TEs. Several more years of positive results from the various TEs are necessary before it can be established that a general trend towards post-communist recovery is on its way.

4.3. Pan-European Integration

In the early stages of post-communism, the collapse of mutual trade between former centrally planned economies sent a violent shock wave through all the region. This mutual trade between the members of the Council of Mutual Economic Assistance (CMEA) comprised some 50-70 per cent of foreign trade in the Eastern European region. CMEA trade was radial in its nature: all CMEA members had intensive trade relations with the Soviet Union while trade between the so called 'small' CMEA countries was relatively unimportant.

After the collapse of the CMEA in 1991, the trade experts of Poland, Czechoslovakia and Hungary started examining the problems involved in developing a new trade accord in Central Eastern Europe. A declaration of co-operation was signed by the leaders of the three countries in Visegrad, Hungary, on February 15, 1991. After that, these countries were called 'The Visegrad Three' or 'The Visegrad Triangle'. Since the beginning of 1993, after the split of Czechoslovakia, the Visegrad group has comprised four countries.

The Visegrad group formed the Central European Co-operation Committee in Budapest, on April 17 1992; a consultative body that provided an institutional framework for mutual economic co-operation. This step was taken after a steep decline in mutual trade which was caused in part by new protective customs regulations introduced after the collapse of the CMEA. These had been put in place in an effort to regulate pricing systems in which production and retail prices were distorted by an assortment of price subsidies encouraging trade in a false direction.

Without going into further details about the emergence of the Visegrad group, it is sufficient to say here that on December 21, 1992, the economic ministers of Poland, the Czech Republic, Slovakia and Hungary signed an agreement in Crakow, Poland, providing for the establishment of a free trade zone between the four signatories. The aim of the agreement, which took effect on March 1, 1993, is to eliminate customs duties between the countries by the year 2001.[58]

The free trade agreement signed reluctantly by the Visegrad quadrangle is obviously an important milestone in the political and economic co-operation of the CEEC region. Unlike the forcibly imposed CMEA, the agreement

---

[58]K Okolicsanyi, 'The Visegrad Free Trade Zone', *RFE/RL Research Report*, No.3, 1993.

to reduce customs duties over a three stage, eight year period is the first truly pragmatic measure to be taken by the now independent and sovereign countries of Central Eastern Europe.

With a market of more than 64 million consumers, the Visegrad region is a new, important factor in the European economy. Jointly, the four states of the new free trade zone will enjoy a much stronger bargaining position in negotiations with the EC over their eventual membership of the community.

It is self-evident that the new trade policy formation of the Visegrad Four is of interest for potential Western investors. All four member states actively pursue an economic policy which involves attracting direct investments from OECD countries. When potential investors decide on the location of their activities in post-communist Europe, the newly established free trade zone of some 64 million inhabitants can hardly be ignored. This fact certainly poses problems for former Soviet republics and former CMEA countries which are not members of the Visegrad zone (Romania and Bulgaria).

The three Baltic states (Estonia, Latvia and Lithuania) formed a free trade area among themselves in 1994. This new trading bloc is much smaller than the 'Visegrad Four' group with only some 8 million inhabitants. Kazakhstan, Uzbekistan and Kyrgyzstan also decided to create a free trade area in 1994. These three former Soviet republics have a combined population of over 40 million.

These trade-policy arrangements within the TE region are certainly of some importance for post-communist countries in their drive to attract FDIs. However, a much more important issue for TEs is to establish viable links with the more affluent part of the old continent. This is not only important for TEs with regard to foreign trade, but also within the framework of FDIs: if goods produced in TEs by Western firms can be freely or relatively freely marketed in Western Europe, the attraction of TEs as host countries for FDIs will increase substantially. There is no unified EU policy towards TEs.

An excellent study on pan-European integration has been written by Professor Richard Baldwin.[59] His work is worth summarizing in this context. According to Baldwin, Pan-European integration is proceeding, despite the fact that no one seems to be in charge. The EU-TE Association Agreements (Europe Agreements which in early 1994 were in force with Poland, Czech Republic, Slovakia, Hungary, Romania and Bulgaria) are important steps. However, these AA-Treaties are bilateral in nature, separately linking each TE to the West European 'hub'.

This 'hub and spoke' bilateralism discourages, in the opinion of Baldwin, foreign and domestic investment in TEs which may slow Eastern growth. West European firms are harmed by the other side of this investment-deterring effect. Trade barriers between TEs - and possibly the future barriers - inhibit normal commercial practices, e.g supplying the region from facilities concentrated in one Eastern country. Intra-TE agreements are an imperfect solution, because investors cannot be sure that these piecemeal deals will become effective.

Baldwin points out that an Eastern enlargement of the EU is improbable for decades, because TEs are simply too poor to be able to find a place in the West European rich men's club. The 64 million people in the Visegrad-4, for ex-

[59]R Baldwin: *Towards and Integrated Europe.* London, 1994.

ample, are 2.5 times more agricultural and only 30 per cent as rich as the EU-12 average. Financing the entry of these four TEs would require drastic cuts in EU spending or a considerable increase in incumbent contributions. Raising taxes or deficits for this would be unpopular with voters. Spending cuts would fall on two extremely powerful interest groups - EU farmers and poor regions, since they receive 80 per cent of EU spending. As a matter of self-defence, coalitions of farmers and poor regions are likely to veto a European enlargement until TEs become much richer and much less agricultural.

In addition to agricultural subsidies and regional transfers, there are two more 'political land mines' (Baldwin) which are stumbling blocks in the EU enlargement eastward: voting issues and migration. Eastern enlargement would turn the EU-voting system upside-down in the Council of Ministers. Free movement of people is likely to cause considerable migration westwards, which is potentially problematic.

Therefore, there are four important reasons why EU membership is not possible for the immediate future, even for the Visegrad countries. Baldwin makes a proposal for the interim period which envisages two phases. The first would redress the hub-and-spoke bilateralism by embedding the existing Europe Agreements into a proposed 'Association of Association Agreements' (AAA). The AAA would require TEs to liberalize equally with all AAA members. The conference of the Treaty of Rome and the proposed AAA would create a duty free zone for industrial goods. Thus, an industrial firm located in any AAA member state would have (after a transitional period) duty free access to any other AAA market. This new framework would promote trade and investment on a pan-European basis. The heightened credibility, consistency and predictability of trade policy throughout the AAA region would be good for European business. The elimination of hub-and-spoke bilateralism should encourage investment in the AAA region.

The second stage in Baldwin's scheme stipulates an intermediate step, called by him an 'Organisation for European Integration' (OEI). The OEI should not replace the AAA since not all TEs would be ready to join simultaneously.

The proposed OEI would help to fulfil the Europe Agreement promise 'to make progress towards realizing between (the EU and each TE) the other economic freedoms on which the community is based.' The OEI Administration should be dominated by the EU and provide assistance in helping potential members from the TE region to adopt community standards on all single market issues. According to Baldwin, the proposed OEI would avoid all four 'political landmines' mentioned above (agriculture, regional help transfers, voting in council of Ministers, and migration). Unlike the AAA, stage two would require no immediate action. Several years must pass before any TE will be ready for an OEI arrangement. Baldwin envisages an inner circle (OEI) comprising all the EU member states plus the leading TEs (not yet EU members) and an outer circle, the AAA, which would delimit the boundary of a European duty free zone for industrial products.

It is naturally impossible to measure the overall investment deterring effect in TEs caused by the lack of a clear pan-European integration scheme and a timetable for its application. Obviously, this effect is smaller in those countries which have been able to conclude 'Europe Agreements' with the EU, than in TEs without them. Trade policy is one of the factors which helps the emergence of uneven development within the TE region. It can be assumed that some sort of hierarchical relationship of EU policy with TEs will continue into the future.

The global economy has been dominated for the past couple of decades by a triad of trading blocs.[60] This Triad comprising North America, Western Europe and Japan, accounts for three quarters of global production, but only one fifth of the global population. Each part of this triad has its own geographical hinterland. J Dunning assumes that at least some of the triad areas will themselves become part of its core, like Taiwan and Korea in Asia and Mexico in America. As more economies become industrialised and better off, the significance of trans-frontier trade and investment, which has always been strongly income-elastic, is likely to increase.[61]

The key question for TEs in the second half of the 1990s and beyond is whether they will be able to integrate themselves into the West European 'hub' of EEA (European Economic Area = EU + EFTA without Switzerland), which has 360 million inhabitants. In this process certain tendencies of the global economy described by Dunning[62] must be taken into consideration. Within both developed and developing economies, too, the role of both producer and consumer services in the value-added process has steadily increased. However, even in the most

---

[60]See K Ohmae: *Triad Power: The Coming Shape of Global Competition* . New York-London, 1985.

[61]J Dunning: *The Globalization of Business.* London-New York, 1993, p.62.

[62]*Ibid.* pp62-63.

advanced industrial countries, it is neither appropriate nor desirable to talk about de-industrialization, notwithstanding the fact that in many developed countries the numbers employed in manufacturing industry has fallen.

The truth is that the interaction between goods and service sectors is becoming increasingly complementary with the one supporting rather than replacing the other. What also seems clear is that the composition of output - be it of goods or services - in the emerging global economy is becoming increasingly determined by the deposition and productivity of 'created' or 'engineered' resources rather than those of 'natural' resources. *Inter alia,* this is shown by the marked fall in the percentage of primary goods and unskilled labour in the value-added of most products.

These tendencies in the global economy are of importance for the development of TEs: the bulk of FDIs take place within the Triad or the 'rich men's club' and reveal a 'herding instinct' which generates uneven development in the global economy. This 'herd' mentality of international business pays less and less attention to blue-collar workers' input and raw material costs; two advantages which are readily available in TEs - although there is an obviously uneven distribution of raw materials within the TE region.

At the same time, it is useful to bear in mind that the systemic change taking place in the East is not creating a market as such on a global scale . TEs must establish economic links to the Triad system by political means, that is by negotiating access to the wealthy part of the Old Continent. Success in this sphere is one of the absolute key ingredients in the transitional process. It is not enough to create academic models of integrating TEs into the system of global economy of trading blocks; these models must also be put into practice.

In the early stage of the systemic change in post-communist countries, representatives of foreign firms came to TEs, where they saw at first hand the low wages and governments' commitment to reform, and they were impressed. However, as shown above, no massive flow of FDIs took place in the early 1990s. According to Dunning,[63] the initial euphoria and the favourable business climate it engendered soon started to wear off. The new mood is reinforced by greater awareness of the practical difficulties posed by investment in the area.

According to one analysis made in the early stage of the transition, the reason for relatively low FDI flow to TEs is simple but important. It is not that the risk-return combination is necessarily unattractive; rather, the explanation for the low levels of FDI arises from the 'option value of waiting'. The expected rate of return to investing, say, in a new plant, may well be higher in Hungary than in France. But there is also very high degree of uncertainty: the transition towards a market economy may splutter and stop; the government may not be able to deliver; or there may be a backlash against foreign investors. Not only the income, but also the capital invested in a TE may be lost. Consequently, firms may find it optimal to wait. The cost of waiting is low.[64]

Leaving aside the uncertainly factor, there is another deterrent to FDIs. It is true that labour costs are low and likely to remain so, based on any reasonable forecast. And

---

[63] *op cit*, p.238.
[64] O Blanchard, R Dornbusch, P Krugman, R Layard and L Summers: '*Reform in Eastern Europe*. Cambridge(Mass)-London, 1991, p.78.

labour costs account at the aggregate level for the majority of costs in value added. But for any particular plant, labour costs account for a relatively small portion of cost, often below 20 per cent, with the bulk of costs coming from intermediate inputs, which themselves embody labour. Thus, large savings in labour costs only come from integrated operations covering many stages of production or from an ability to buy inputs from other firms within the country or economic area. These in turn require the existence of a reliable communication and transportation system. What is urgently needed is a sophisticated infrastructure, from telecommunications to transportation, which does not exist at this stage in TEs. It is crucial to put in place such an infrastructure quickly, even if it requires foreign borrowing.[65]

While TEs need to invest in infrastructure, industry, efficient public sector administration, and modern financial systems, large portions of government resources are tied up in debt service (internal and external debt), entitlement programmes, and subsidies - not a unique situation in the global economy. In many TEs, the external creditworthiness is questionable, and this means that there is only limited access to external financial markets, even after some rescheduling of previous debts has taken place. Unfortunately for TEs, no 'grand scheme ' resembling the 'Marshall Plan' has been established to help them to bring their infrastructure up to the Western level.

There are, therefore, a series of factors which hamper the inflow of FDIs in TEs: trade-policy matters, with country-differences; inadequate infrastructure linked with difficulties to finance its improvement; low local purchasing

[65]*ibid.*, pp.80-81.

power inherited from communist time and aggravated by the post-communist slump and accompanied by considerable social tension; and difficulties in establishing macroeconomic equilibrium (with clear differences in each of the various TEs).

These factors taken together have created a situation in which the political mood is radically changing from that of the early stage of transition. 'Post-communist parties' - successor organizations of old power structures - are gaining ground, as pointed out above. In 1994, the Reformed Communist party of Ukraine became the biggest faction in parliamentary elections - without gaining an absolute majority. In Hungary the Socialist Party was expected to do well in elections but the fact that they obtained an absolute majority came as a surprise to many observers.

It is not possible to predict the consequences and to draw scenarios of the election victories of democratic left forces in various TEs. It suffices to state here that the visible tendency of neo-communist or socialist groupings to return to political power in TEs is certainly not a factor enhancing TEs chances of receiving badly needed FDIs, even although no one is suggesting that the new left parties will return to communism during the second half of the 1990s, or after. It is however, psychologically difficult to convince the Western business community that TEs can provide a favourable 'investment climate' with socialist governments or governments strongly influenced by socialist parliamentary groups.

There are obviously several real and intangible factors which are apparently deterring large-scale FDIs from taking place in TEs in the second half of the 1990s. At the same time, however, this does not mean that incentives to invest in TEs are missing altogether.

As pointed out above, several billion dollars worth of FDIs took place in TEs during the extremely severe slump of the immediate post-communist period. This investment flow occurred in spite of the recession in the OECD region.

Some TEs are in the mid-1990s poised to start an economic upturn (Poland, Czech Republic, Hungary) with reasonable macro-economic stability. Also some former Soviet republics, especially Estonia and Latvia, have been able to bring their economy under reasonable macro-economic stability.

Therefore, it can be assumed that the 'fast reforming countries (FRCs) will be able to receive an increasing inflow of FDIs if economic prospects in host countries have an influence in FDI decisions. In the long run, certain natural riches in several TEs have an attraction for foreign investors.

One undisputed inducement in all TEs is cheap labour, combined with a labour market where there is a relatively high education level and rather high open or hidden unemployment. This scenario provides many advantages for potential foreign employers in TEs.

Average monthly wages are really extremely low when compared with those in Western countries, as the figures in the table below show.[66]

---

66 (Sandor Richter: *East-West Trade Under Growing Western Protectionism*, WIIW (Vienna, Forschungsbericht No 198, June 1993).

Average gross monthly wages 1992 in US$

Hungary	283
Poland	219
Czechoslovakia	164
Bulgaria	88
Romania	64
Austria	2760
Germany (West)	3191

The difference between East and West is striking. In Hungary, where the wages are the highest within the TE-region, the average gross pay is only about 10 oer cent of the Austrian level which is lower than in Germany (West). In Romania it is possible to hire around fortythree workers for a month for the average pay of one Austrian worker.

Therefore, one can maintain that there are clear incentives, in the labour-intensive branches of industry, to shift production from the West to the East. However, not only wages but also labour productivity must be taken into consideration and labour costs per unit of output calculated.

It is a well-known fact that productivity levels are much lower in the East than in the West. However, productivity may improve spectacularly if new technologies are imported within the framework of FDIs. Hence, there are numerous attractive business opportunities in which new technology can be coupled with cheap Eastern labour which is in ample supply. This should prove relatively advantageous for many years to come. It can be assumed that inflation in the post-communist countries tends to be higher than in the OECD-countries and this can create pressure for regular devaluation of Eastern currencies. This likely scenario means that labour costs in the East will remain relatively attractive for the foreseeable future.

It is also well-recognized that labour costs are no longer decisive for the manufacturing industries. According to present international comparisons, the labour component in manufacturing costs is only in the region of 10-15 per cent of total costs. Therefore, cheap labour is not necessarily a dominant factor in direct capital investments.

There are some interesting details in the labour-cost table above concerning the relative position of TEs. In Hungary labour costs are, according to the figures given by WIIW, about twice as expensive as those in former Czechoslovakia. This implies that labour productivity is twice as high in Hungary as in former Czechoslovakia. This is not necessarily the case. Obviously, there are some biases in the exchange rates (ERs).

In the early years of transition the Hungarian forint was clearly 'over-valued' in comparison to the Czechoslovakian and later Czech crown. In other words, the Hungarian forint has been relatively less grossly undervalued vis-a-vis Western currencies than the Czech crown (koruna).

From the point of view of FDIs this means that labour costs (calculated in Western currencies) are extremely low in the Czech Republic due to ER undervaluation. Therefore, there are labour-cost differences among TEs which can be surprising.

It is evident that TEs have cheap labour in European comparison but this does not mean that they have an absolute advantage in the global market. John Anthony, managing director of APV Hungary, the British food-processing machinery manufacturers, is impressed with the quality of skilled labour in Hungary, but says that you would have to keep moving eastward if you wanted to keep up with cheap labour costs: 'People bang the drum about Hungary being a low-cost manufacturing base, but I think that is irrelevant. If you are up against the Chinese and they are going to be on a dollar a day for the next 20 years, then Hungary is not a competitor in those kind of terms'.[67]

This statement which refers to Hungary as a location of relatively but not absolutely cheap labour is of importance for all TEs. Goods can now be made everywhere and sold anywhere, and more and more services can be performed at great distance. There is an ever expanding global labour pool as more than 47 million people enter the job market each year. Production becomes more efficient in an economic sense, but the next generation faces declining prospects of stable, well-paid jobs, and there is a real danger that more of the world's's population are fated to be window shoppers, not customers.[68]

There is therefore a real long-term problem for TEs: they have all relatively cheap labour easily available for the use of foreign investors, but cheap (even cheaper) labour is extensively offered. Low income levels mean that the majority of the TEs' populations must be satisfied with lots of window-shopping but very limited real consumption. This is one of the reasons why socialist (ex-communist) groupings have been so successful in TEs after some

---

[67] *Business Central Europe*, April 1994, p.35.

[68] R Barnet - J Cavanagh: *Global Dreams: Imperial Corporations and the New World Order*. New York-London-Toronto-Sydney-Tokyo-Singapore, 1994, p.420

years of transition: the change brought about by systemic corrections has created a new economic environment in the visual sense, rather than in concrete terms. Newer and better items are on offer, but only certain sections of the society can afford them.

Conclusions

The first days and weeks of post-communism were full of optimism and euphoria which soon melted away as it became clear that systemic cha nge in the East could not be carried out quickly and painlessly. The pain caused by the post-communist slump has been worse than commonly was anticipated.

Soon the honeymoon with the market romanticism was over in TEs, and it was replaced by frustrations and doomsday forecasts in which it was stated that capitalism in TEs cannot be created without capital. Dark pessimism became prevalent.

In the middle of the 1990s it has become clear that the extremely optimistic and pessimistic predictions have started to look outdated. Clear benefits resulting from the immediate post-communist pains have become discernible. These gains are not evenly divided throughout the TE region; reasonable stabilization has not been reached everywhere. The many changes in the political scene have often been difficult for outsiders to predict.

However, TEs have some favourable cards up their sleeves for the second half of the decade. Each of them has a cheap and well-educated labour force which has always been a positive factor from the point of view of foreign investors.

The majority of TE equities are, in the eyes of foreign investors, either cheap or extremely cheap. Therefore, it can be assumed that equities in these emerging markets will be bought. Naturally, the 'real' values of these assets are difficult to estimate and new stock exchanges are extremely volatile. Still, portfolio investors are moving into the TE casino-like exchange places. Obviously, winners will make huge fortunes, while losers will get their fingers burnt.

The cumulative effect of FDIs in certain TEs is clear to see. When one company moves in, it probably creates demand in the local economy which will be satisfied by newcomers. A virtuous circle of investment can thus come into being.

There are also some obviously negative ingredients in the TE investment climate. Rules and regulations are often unclear and they change continuously. Law enforcement is an obvious bottleneck. Stories about increasing crime rates are not necessarily untrue. There is plenty of red tape left. Social tension is high and strikes not uncommon. There are huge inadequacies in the infrastructure, especially with regard to telecommunications. Average earnings are extremely low and, as a result, purchasing power is far below West European levels. Although there are many educated people, they are not necessarily familiar with Western management methods. And the environmental damage caused under communism is in many places quite appalling.

In spite of these obviously negative considerations, it is highly likely that in the second half of the 1990s, as economic growth gains momentum in the TE region, Western natural and juridical persons will become more and more involved in TE development via portfolio investments and FDIs. Western investors have shown interest already, during the difficult early years of transition. In the coming years of certainty a myriad of deals in TEs will be concluded, making the TE region one of the most interesting places among the 'emerging markets'.

Communists got their economics entirely wrong: they maximized costs and minimized private consumption; while they caused unprecedented damage to the natural environment. Entrepreneurial spirit was meant to be eliminated completely; but it re-emerged in the 'black market' without which the official economy would have been unable to function. This system of central planning belongs in the dustbin of economic history.

There is no real chance of Soviet central planning rising Phoenix-like from the ashes. Theoretically, the old system of Soviet planning can only be re-established in Russia, which still has an abundance of natural resources on her territory. Smaller TEs simply cannot function with an extremely wasteful system as they do not have sufficient resources to waste. Therefore, successor parties to the communists cannot go back to the old system even if they wanted. Indeed, there is very little evidence that ex-communist politicians in Lithuania, Poland or Hungary even have the slightest wish to go back to the 'good old days' of communism.

In the current era, with the globalisation of monetary and capital markets, national governments everywhere have suffered the loss of economic sovereignty. It is now difficult for governments to act in isolation. Local autocrats, who once enjoyed cold-war political subsidies from superpowers, now find that the till drains quickly; if economic and political stability is not established, capital flight takes place.

This new emphasis on economic equilibrium is particularly important for TEs, as international investors are needed to help service the potential (and actual) budget and trade deficits. This fact has lessened the room for manoeuvre in TE economic policy-making.

This all does not necessarily mean that all populist elements in post-communist policy-making in fifteen former Soviet republics and six European ex-CMEA member countries will disappear overnight and that pragmatism with optimal macro-economic management will be applied everywhere without any friction. It is highly likely that the TE region of twenty one countries, will present a diversified picture of economic development, during which foreign investors must make careful research before risking their money. It is a fairly safe bet that capital inflow into the TE region will be distributed unevenly among the various post-communist countries.

Index

D

E

F

G

H

I

J & L

M

N & O

T

U, V & W